Also available at all good book stores

9781785316852

9781785316265

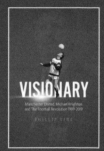

9781785315770

9781785315541

9781785314476

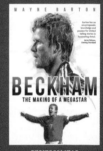

9781785316760

9781785314698

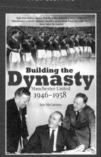

9781785313974

9781785310041

INGLORY
INGLORY
MAN UNITED

INGLORY
INGLORY
MAN UNITED
TRAVELS AND TRAVAILS OF A
1980s RED DEVIL

JAMIE MAGILL

First published by Pitch Publishing, 2021

Pitch Publishing
A2 Yeoman Gate
Yeoman Way
Worthing
Sussex
BN13 3QZ
www.pitchpublishing.co.uk
info@pitchpublishing.co.uk

ISBN 978 1 78531 816 0

Typesetting and origination by Pitch Publishing
Printed and bound in India by Replika Press Pvt. Ltd.

Contents

Act 1.   Isn't It a Pity? 9

Act 2.   Beware of Darkness 15

Act 3.   Plug Me In 35

Act 4.   I'd Have You Anytime 52

Act 5.   Out of the Blue 69

Act 6.   It's What You Value 86

Act 6a.   I Remember Jeep 108

Act 7.   Hear Me Lord 126

Act 8.   I Live For You 146

Act 9.   Awaiting On You All 165

Act 10.   Behind That Locked Door 180

Act 11.   Arnold Grove 197

Act 12.   Cockamamie Business 210

Act 12a. Fish on the Sand 222

Act 13.   Unknown Delight 230

Act 14.   And in the End … 252

To Steve,

For the pills and thrills and bellyaches, the good papers, the bad tea, the Safeway cider – above all, your ace tunes, love and company.

Lots of love from Jamie.

Act 1

Isn't It a Pity?

Before we start on all the United stuff (it is United by the way; anyone who calls us Manchester or Man U should probably not be reading this book), let me ask you one question: what year do you wish you were born? It's a cracking question isn't it? And it makes me wonder why no one ever asks it. There are so many opportunities: wet weekends, village fetes, barbecues, dinner parties, Zoom socials, yet no one takes them up. I blame the petits bourgeois myself: they do not have the intellect or imagination to ask anything important; nor do they have the social confidence to be truly honest. So instead we hear about tomorrow's make-or-break PowerPoint, the caravan in Rhyl and the buy-to-let property in Cyprus that has not been built yet, and never will.

So? What year do you wish you were born? Me? I would have been a baby boomer of 1947 vintage to properly embrace Beatlemania – perfect G, D, Em, Am (and maybe C for the middle eight as F is too much like hard work) by 10am, clear it with the church by lunchtime and conquer

America before mac and cheese and root beer for tea. The year 1919 too. Picture it: an 11-year-old, queuing outside Headingley with nothing more than a stale roll, a scorecard and a clearly etched vision of Bradman strolling to the crease at first drop. Batting all day. Breaking records. That's history. Well worth that special brand of arse-wrecking, wooden-bench soreness that only the true fan knows; these were the halcyon days of the genuine enthusiast. Proper lads who viewed a cricket ground as somewhere between a place of worship and an Alsatia. No dilettantes. No corporate whores. In fact, not a plush bucket seat or a pop-up restaurant in sight.

Back on planet earth, I am quietly content with my 1975. And I say that as a United fan. Football defines you between seven and 14 before women, money and children turn you into a sycophantic hypocrite. So, in substance, those years are all that count in anyone's existence. In my 1980s wet breaks were football quizzes, and dry breaks were Bryan Robson in midfield or Sparky Hughes up front and not giving a shit about scuffed-up Clarks or minor radioactive drizzle. Weekends were back-to-back club games with no thought of rest and rotation: recovery time only allowed you to go half-blind, half-crazy with a wordsearch competition hoping that a pair of Nike boots in the *Shoot!* magazine might be yours. They were the best times; save hearing your young kids sing Beatles songs, nothing gets remotely near.

School holidays were an excuse to kit up and show off, piss your dad off with endless questions from your *Playfair Football Annual* and sleep with the ball. So how can I be happy with 1975 when between 1983 and 1989 we won next to nothing? And that lot up the M62 hoovered up at home better than Shake n' Vac and did better than Napoleon in Europe? Am I crazy? Quite possibly. But Nick Mahoney was a United fan. He was the captain and our best player at Grappenhall Sports which was a huge factor, but it was more than that. On our club summer trip (always a day out at Blackpool) he was first to brave the Monster Drop at Peabody's; he rode backwards into the Black Hole at Derby Baths and beltless on the Grand National at the Pleasure Beach; this was all after a hundredweight of sausage and chips in the clubhouse and a gallon of shit pop. He had also worked out in the scrummage for proper coke hastily handed out by those in charge at the front of the coach that if you pulled up one sleeve and crossed your hands you were guaranteed two cans with the certainty of tides and school the day after Sunday. And the Liverpool fans in the Grappenhall Sports brethren? Well, they were more ball pool and carousel: the types who would dozily bust their mouths on fairground mirrors and bleat about the salty chips later on. Dave Hobbs was a Liverpool fan and he would not let go of the assistant on the Monster Drop. He is probably still there now – about 50ft long. So, we have the United Cavalier or the Liverpool Roundhead? The dull religion of Anfield or the enlightenment of Old Trafford? The establishment red or the romantic red devil. You decide …

The 1980s was a decade of true inglory for United fans. I can remember the game at Old Trafford against Crystal Palace in December 1989. These were the days of 'Fergie Out' banners (yes, really). Fergie didn't help himself that day by leaving out Mark Hughes (yes, really) and playing Lee Sharpe up front instead but when Palace (who had been eviscerated 9-0 at Anfield just a few months earlier) equalised that day we all knew we were going to lose. Against Crystal Palace at home. That was some kind of shit-stained nadir. It's no longer catatonic shock and horror which you can deal with; it's acceptance that Geoff Thomas was man of the match and there's nothing you can do about it. Old Trafford was not the Theatre of Dreams back then; it was more like the dark, satanic mills of some ghoulish Victorian nightmare. Some lost interest and took up gridiron or golf or stockbroking or backgammon; some turned to the dark side – Liverpool; some lost jobs; some lost partners; some lost homes. Fuck them – no balls. The ones that mattered never lost hope. Don't moan when you lose and don't brag when you win: learning to deal with the twin imposters of success and failure is a metaphor for life and United back then were the best training out there. You survive the bad times hoping for more favourable interest rates, a better job, a more attractive girl, a bigger house, and if you bide your time, you never know, Eric Cantona may turn up. The outrageous, the bad and the ugly build resilience and character: remember just because you are, or think you are, or may indeed be, a character doesn't mean you have any. At least fame didn't change the swashbuckling Grappenhall Sports captain of 1983 – Nick Mahoney converted to rugby union, owns his own talent coaching agency and lives close to Kate Moss and Liam Gallagher in Hampstead. Who said you can tell the winners at the starting post?

Of course, the United fans born in 1983 missed all of this. I doubt they really believe that the United holocaust of the early 1980s actually happened save in some badly preserved YouTube download, the authenticity of which can always be challenged. All this generation know is uninterrupted success and what can you learn from silver and gold save how to spend it and acquire plastic friends? Oh, and please don't mention David Moyes or Louis van Gaal or Mourinho or even Ole for that matter – one, or two, slightly over-plump bin bags do not the winter of discontent make. Try finishing 11th and having your season over on 4 January every other year. Then you'll know the football equivalent of freezing cold without a snorkel parka; a battle for a Champions League spot and a few semi-finals is a nice warm Radox bath in comparison. To take your seat on the United grand jury you need to be balanced and objective in the mania of your deepest prejudices: rose-coloured Ryan Giggs spectacles are fine as long as they do not totally obscure the bulging cataracts of Ralph Milne.

So perhaps, after all, 1975 was a good year to be born for United fans. All those life skills it taught us! Maybe there is more to it than meets the eye. I am not going to bore anyone with my cack-handed musings over normative ethics, but it does seem to me that to enjoy pleasure you need to experience pain. But, in reality, all true football fans (not the ones who ask about Beckham or the offside rule during a crucial World Cup qualifier) are crypto sadomasochists anyway – we love nothing more than the idea of disembowelling the misfiring centre-forward, immersing the arrogant manager in molten lava, or burying the parsimonious owner alive. If it takes a home defeat to Coventry City to reach this spiritual nirvana, then so be it.

I bet de Sade would love all of this. Maybe he was a United fan? The first Red Devil? These scribblings would give him plenty of material for experimental pleasure. If you've not worked it out already, this book focuses on 1983–90 when we were far from fab. It was tough back then you know; it wasn't all Marmalade Atkins, Super Noodles and Jimmy White.

Act 2

Beware of Darkness

To celebrate the mediocre is a crime, and, if it isn't, it ought to be – Warrington, Cheshire (formerly Lancashire) is an interesting case study. For those sages in our midst who drive straight through, take a look at Warrington's most famous sons (and daughters): Jesse Lingard, Steven Arnold (before you ask, he played Ashley in Corrie), Kerry Katona, Rebekah Brooks. It's a who's who alright. But for every newspaper chief and perma-tan reality TV star there's an Ian Brown, a Roger Hunt, a Chris Evans and a Louisa from Grappenhall. Did I tell you that the armies of Oliver Cromwell and the Earl of Derby once stayed in Warrington? I bet it was for only one night. Maybe the IKEA was closed, and they had to march on warts and all without the fortification of crisp hot dogs and first-rate ice cream? How the social history of England might have been different ...

Back in 1983 Warrington did offer one unlikely crumb of solace: it gave you a legitimate reason to support Liverpool. I reckon half of the kids did back then, with the residue mainly United with a bit of City and Everton thrown in – of course there was the odd clown who purported to support Spurs but he was usually recaptured quite soon as he protested in vain that Glenn Hoddle was the Second Coming. And why not support Liverpool? They were First Division champions after all. School playgrounds make America look democratic, so you do what you have to do to give you that edge. It's all about being first at school: you want to be first pick at break time, first in line at the Panini stickers swap shop ('Got!', 'Got!', 'Got!', when really all you have is the free packet that came with the *Shoot!* magazine the previous summer), first to stamp the marrow out of veteran conkers, first in the queue for Mild Curry crisps at morning break, first at the ice cream van for the super sour jawbreakers and Wham bars, first in the school strip at afternoon break if you're good enough or lucky enough to be selected for the school team. Get the picture? Football was currency back then – well before button pushing spoilt life for us it was the passport to legitimacy and acceptance. In that context, supporting the best team in the land clearly helped.

Nick Mahoney showed me the United way but that's only part of the background. I'll say this very quietly, but I started off as a City fan. Yes, there are pictures of me in 1982 in City strips. The light blue one. The black and red vertical stripes away kit. My dad was a blue you see. So, what happened? Two words. Raddy Antić. On 14 May 1983 City only needed a point at home to Luton Town to stay in the First Division. Luton needed a win to achieve the same purpose. With five minutes remaining it was 0-0 and Dad and I were glued to *World of Sport*. He was too nervous to listen live on the wireless (he never called it the radio) and these were pre-Teletext days, so we had to make do with the score flashes on *World of Sport*. They were sometimes hard to notice in between the huge torsos of Giant Haystacks and Big Daddy and the bouffant of Dickie Davies. But this one wasn't: MANCHESTER CITY 0 LUTON 1. 'Fucking hell!' was all Dad said. We quickly turned to *Grandstand* (well I did as this was my job pre-remote control) and then the vidiprinter confirmed City's fate. I think there were a few more 'fucking hells' before the bacon and Super Noodles we had for tea half an hour later. A few Harp Lagers before *Juliet Bravo* calmed him down.

Anyway, what was I supposed to do? It's a bit like Matt Le Tissier has said about why he didn't leave Southampton. As long as they were in the top flight, he was OK. Same with me, but the Second Division? No bloody chance. Imagine that in the playground. 'Who you got this weekend Jamie?' 'Oh, we've got Cambridge United away. They could be tough to break down.' It was enough to get your head kicked in at our school. Everyone stayed away from one lad at school. You must remember that lad? If Paul Wood found out I was supporting a Second Division team then I would get a proper working over. Just a few months earlier John Kelly's prize for inadvertently stepping on Woody's spanking new Dunlop Green Flash was to have shit stuffed in his Yamaha recorder. That put an abrupt end to Mrs Sudlow's winter concert – in front of the parents and governors as well. Another lad nicked his Choc Dips and can of Top Deck lemonade shandy and lived to regret it. I learnt very early in life that physical bravery is for the foolhardy and dumb: don't encourage attention from the idiots (for example, by supporting a shit team) and if they do come your way then agree to lend them your BMX, your ZX81 and your sister. They'll have forgotten in the morning and will be on their next mission.

Dad probably didn't care that much about my egregious act of treachery; at least he didn't show it, but thankfully his generation didn't feel compelled to tell the world and his wife each time they went to Tesco and bought a box of eggs with one cracked. Maybe he was hurt? Thirty odd years later I told my son that Spurs was fine, but if he went with Liverpool or Chelsea, I'd never speak to him again. Well? Fair's fair, isn't it? It was a massive thing for me though. I felt a touch of shame when on 15 May 1983 (a day after the relegation) I took down my pictures of David Cross, Dennis Tueart and Kevin Reeves and replaced them with Norman Whiteside, Bryan Robson and Frank Stapleton. Dad hadn't even come to terms with the divorce and I moved a fitter bird into my room the very next day. I didn't even close the door as she shamelessly cavorted around in a number of outfits. Announcing it to my friends was the easy bit: half of them were United fans anyway and the Liverpool lot could now take the piss even more. They could say what they liked: it was the FA Cup Final the very next week. Manchester United v Brighton and Hove Albion. My first game would be at Wembley Stadium in front of 100,000 for the biggest prize in football. Oh, I can feel your grumblings and glory boy asides from here in sunny N5!

I know the concept has been force-fed to death in recent years but in 1983 the FA Cup was the apotheosis of football; on balance, it was probably more important than the First Division and, most definitely, preferable to European glory. Why? Because it told a good story: the artisans Brighton and Hove Albion meet the aristocrats of Manchester United on remotely even terms on a one-off, winner-takes-all occasion when anything is possible. OK, I will say it but just once: David v Goliath. But what's not to like about that anyway? And that was just the final itself. We had the mud and ice of the January third round (punctuated by the story shown on *Grandstand* of the part-time postman/butcher/baker/window cleaner/sandwich spreader/delivery man from Crewe frothing at the prospect of shaking Ian Rush's hand), the possibility of endless replays and late school-night highlights and the nerve tingling anticipation of the April Villa Park semi-finals. Cup final day in the 1980s – a huge event: football's Royal Ascot, Wimbledon final and Lord's Saturday rolled into one.

In keeping with the gravitas of the occasion, the build-up started around 9am on both channels (saving a grateful nation from its weekly penance at the altar of Keith Chegwin, Maggie Philbin and Bob Carolgees) and meandered quite delightfully towards 'Abide With Me'. I can remember I was deprived of this. Dad took us to town shopping for a Laura Ashley dress for Mum and to Marks & Spencer; maybe he was raging at me. Or he was showing me and my sister how deliciously middle class he had become with his credit card and Cavalier company car and tape deck stuffed with Phil Collins and Dire Straits. You know, in the 'football no longer matters to me' sense? Where's the antiques fair and the garden party?

United finished the 1982/83 season in third position – 12 points behind the champions Liverpool. Not bad you think? Well, before you get carried away, we (I can say we now by the way) were one point behind Elton John's Watford who had only been promoted to the First Division that year and five years earlier were in the Fourth Division – the lowest tier of the Football League. A United win was more certain than death and taxation. But neither the Grim Reaper nor the VAT man was about to spoil a bloody good day out. As Jimmy Case (of Liverpool fame), who played for Brighton that day, recalled in a MailOnline interview in 2010:

> There was something about the Cup that season. We weren't very good in the league but when it came to the Cup, the whole town came alive. We just ran it as far as we could.
>
> We were a bunch of jokers. We knew we were the underdogs against United but we were those types of characters anyway. Before the final, we had a lunch and this comedian, Bob 'the Cat' Bevan, who was a Brighton fan, came in and did a show for us before we got on the helicopter.

At least we had our own comedian in Ron Atkinson. These the days before the cult of management personality infected the mainstream: now we know all about Jürgen's glasses and teeth and favourite pasta and the boxing training of his landlord Brendan, but back then their contribution to the media was pretty laconic: there was pretty much nothing apart from the odd 'All credit to the lads John; this is always a hard place to come but they done great today' on *Match of the Day*. But the media Ron we knew in the 90s does shed some light on what might have been going on in that dressing room at Wembley around 2pm on the afternoon of 21 May 1983. You can see him putting his bejewelled arm around Arnold Mühren and imploring the cultured left footer to 'put in some spongy balls for Frank Stapleton' and 'get it to the back stick early doors'. Over to Ray Wilkins: 'Butch, it's about the two Ms today – movement and passing.' No doubt we would have been 'firing on all cylinders' with that steak and suet ready to burn.

The team that day was as below:

1. Gary Bailey
2. Mike Duxbury
3. Arthur Albiston
4. Ray Wilkins
5. Kevin Moran
6. Gordon McQueen
7. Bryan Robson (captain)
8. Arnold Mühren
9. Frank Stapleton
10. Norman Whiteside
11. Alan Davies

Substitute:
12. Ashley Grimes.

Alan Davies? I know what you're thinking. Big Ron had signed Lawrie Cunningham on loan from Real Madrid that April, but he was struggling with injury. Some player him and he played for England just six times. I hummed unconvincingly to 'Abide With Me'. Even now I don't know any of the words. Do any football fans? Does anyone? What exactly are they singing/mumbling/humming? So, here's the moment every football fan has been waiting for since circa 1927:

Abide with Me
Abide with me, fast falls the eventide
The darkness deepens Lord, with me abide
When other helpers fail and comforts flee
Help of the helpless, oh, abide with me

Swift to its close ebbs out life's little day
Earth's joys grow dim, its glories pass away
Change and decay in all around I see
O Thou who changest not, abide with me

I fear no foe, with Thee at hand to bless
Ills have no weight, and tears no bitterness
Where is death's sting?
Where, grave, thy victory?
I triumph still, if Thou abide with me

Hold Thou Thy cross before my closing eyes
Shine through the gloom and point me to the
    skies
Heaven's morning breaks, and earth's vain
    shadows flee
In life, in death, o Lord, abide with me
Abide with me, abide with me

Songwriters: Henry Francis Lyte/Will Henry Monk
'Abide With Me' *lyrics Universal Music Publishing Group, Kobalt Music Publishing Ltd.*

Pretty moving isn't it, even on an implacable November afternoon in Highbury N5. Bet you feel better now? Bookmark this page for next year's cup final, if we have one that is. But at least the confusion of 100,000 souls at Wembley was drowned out by Dad's savage and, sadly for me, solo onslaught on confectionery ranging from American Hard Gums (harder back then) to Midget Gems through to Liquorice Torpedoes and white and then strawberry Bonbons (he didn't like the lemon ones). In between the infernal din were censorious asides about Atkinson 'swine', Wilkins 'pudding', Bailey 'sunbed' and, no doubt, others.

As kick-off approached and the fantastic Adidas tracksuit tops were shorn, I suddenly felt a sense of belonging. I guess at eight you only belong to things which impress superficially and while I felt a pang of guilt it didn't register on the Richter scale. Where was I in February when United were struggling in the fifth round away at Derby County at the Baseball Ground on that shit tip of a glue-pot pitch? Was I sweating at Villa Park in the semi-final when Tony Woodcock put the Gunners 1-0 up? Did I care? No, not really. There were nerves though. When City lost, the playground mafia just plain did not care, or notice. It was different with United. Losing to Brighton would be unbearable and the Liverpool contingent would never let us forget. But for Simon Stone (rabid Liverpool fan of the worst kind even now) the consequences of a United win were even more dire, for back in February in front of any number of witnesses he had promised to 'show his arse at Market Gate if United won the cup'.

Nature wreaked its only infernal revenge on Bertie Bassett. Around 2.45pm the heavens opened in Warrington. My dad was far from impressed; he was already two parts into his third Harp Lager top and while he always did what he wanted ('There's only one person steering this ship and that's me. And if you don't like the direction in which it's heading then get off it.') he hated any form of 'mither', so he had absolutely no choice other than to brave the elements – pretending the peg bag was Gary Bailey's head. He had some work friends round at 5 for a game of snooker on the 6 x 3 table so he wanted the leg break of a United FA Cup win to be a clean and crisp one. The snooker was important. These were the halcyon days of Steve Davis, Hurricane Higgins, Whirlwind White. And Bill Werbeniuk supping crates and crates of ale on the job. It was a status symbol too: anyone with a 6 x 3 table with net pockets and a spider rest was going places.

Because it would only take 90 minutes, wouldn't it? The painstakingly prepared and wide-ranging medley of banners (a deeply rich but sadly bygone part of the FA Cup Final tapestry) established a consensus of sorts: 'MORAN – A CUT ABOVE THE REST' seemed to resonate more than the less convincing 'WE'LL PUT WHITESIDE ON HIS BACKSIDE'. No prematch handshakes save with the royals (what a fine waste of time they both are); no diving; no histrionics; no tactical substitutions; no Gatorade or energy gels; no wanton dissent: I know life and society has moved on but we can still learn lots from the design aesthetics of a Wright Brothers plane and Donovan and

The Ink Spots are as cool now as they ever were. In front 2-1 courtesy of a sublime left-foot curler from the unlikely source of Ray Wilkins, United were home and hosed. Ten minutes or so remained. Robson was imperious; his mere presence ensured shape, balance and order and inspired confidence, even amongst the wan-faced, battle-scarred supporters. The number 7 on his back was a metaphor for the mole on my dad's face on a long car journey – no matter how treacherous the terrain, how unrelenting the elements, the mole would get you to safety, and repel everything from sleet to hail, from fire to brimstone, from Barcelona to Liverpool via Brighton and Hove Albion.

But when someone slams the brakes on in thick, pea-soup traffic what can one do? The equaliser came through Gary Stevens with minutes left on the clock – I would never trust my old man again, but I would always find a way to forgive Robson. On a bog of a Wembley surface (these were the days long before Freddie Mercury when Evel Knievel would merrily hack away at the hallowed turf and what little he left would be gaily eviscerated by Princess Anne and her equine lot) United were done, and extra time seemed a punishment prescribed by Beelzebub himself. You don't see it so much these days but back then extra time was like the Somme battlefield – shell-shocked men plodding forlornly forward, armour (shin guards) shorn, socks rolled to jackboots; this was the final push, over the top, mind over matter, will to win. The growing number of casualties succumbed to muscle-knotting cramps and looked desperately to the bench for medical discharge, but the one sub had been on since the 55th minute and Wembley was no place to desert.

There seemed slightly more life in Brighton – maybe it was the sea air or the fish diet or the sprightly night scene, but they pressed forward with greater purpose. And then? Gordon Smith. Clean through. Seconds left. He must score. I can see it now. Bailey made a fine half-stop with his legs and then clung on to the loose ball as if it was an orphaned koala. A replay secured. People criticise replays which seems a little odd in today's age of mental-health awareness. Replays made sure I lived beyond the age of 15. I would probably have killed myself if we had lost a cup final on penalties. I told my dad 'I feel like I have kicked every ball' and he smiled. An unprompted cliché at the age of eight shows you are a lifelong member of the club every dad wants his son to be part of. I remember being pissed up in Altrincham in 2005 watching the Ashes and my mates and I spotted Norman Whiteside. So, I go up to him and ask about the 83 final and whether we underestimated Brighton? I know it was a shit question, but it was the first thing that came into my head. 'Fuck off' was his reply. In an interview with Newstalk on 19 May 2018, when asked the same question, he was a little more forthcoming:

> I don't think we did actually. I just think it was a poor performance and that can happen.
>
> We had looked over so many FA Cup Final games and every year it's not the best game of football because sometimes they become an anti-climax and I've heard that commentated many times but we just went into it hopeful we were going to play well but it never turned out that way and Brighton gave us a really good run for our money.

Maybe Big Norm is sick of answering this question or he was more interested in the blonde he was with?

United won the replay 4-0 and, aside from the early goals and the deeply unfathomable concept of how the same game can start in broad daylight and end in pitch black, my most vivid memory, strangely, was Norman Whiteside drinking milk in the post-match interviews. 'Why not Coca-Cola?' I thought. I didn't think that for long. Good bit of work from the Milk Marketing Board. Mind you, with Thatcher taking it away from the kids they needed to target a new demographic.

But what if Smith had scored? Simon Stone did show his arse at Market Gate – but we only have his word for that. And this is the kid who swore blind that he did meet you as planned at 6am at the M56 services to go to Chester Zoo and further lamented that he had to flour bomb the warders, fight the chimpanzees, strap rubber on the water buffalo and watch the elephants shit bricks all alone. If Smith had scored, I may have gone back to City and you would have been spared all this nonsense. Robson may have gone – Juventus and Sampdoria went in for him that summer and without silverware and the old 'cup winners make strong title challengers next term' syndrome, which was prevalent back then, the allure of the land of sunshine and pasta may have been irresistible. What about Big Ron? This would have been two years in the job with no trophy. And to lose to Brighton deserves some punishment surely? Maybe we would have got someone more stout than champagne, perhaps Ferguson slightly early. But he has just beaten Real Madrid with Aberdeen in a European final so why would he swap that for the dross of a faded giant? What about Cloughie? That would have been fun; but the best girlfriends are fun, until they are not. Unlike Ferguson I think his best days were behind him. Maybe if that éminence grise Peter Taylor had joined him it could have been different but they were estranged by then. With Taylor who knows? Keep Peter Beardsley and David Platt, buy a young Gary Lineker and we may not have had to wait until 1993 for a title. Anyway, hindsight is an easy vantage point. And there again we could have got Jock Stein or Billy McNeill.

I was basking in the watery late-spring sunshine of success. I played like Maradona the day after at school. Maradona in a Bryan Robson shirt. I felt like I improved as a player. I was already on the school team and featured for a local junior side and somehow my volte-face towards United instilled me with greater confidence on the park. I felt like a player returning to his club side after his first England cap. Of course this had nothing to do with an improvement in size, skill or tactical acumen but if you play as Kevin Reeves on the playground you perhaps, subconsciously, believe you are Kevin Reeves when you cross the white line. If, suddenly, you become Bryan Robson three times a day (and again after school), same thing. I was now drumming in Monaco not Macclesfield. Confidence is so easy to acquire when you are a kid. Maybe I should pretend to be George Carman or T.S. Eliot when I wake up tomorrow and I'll be in Cannes this time next year.

It wasn't long before I added a Charity Shield winners' gong to my collection. We had started training at Grappenhall Sports early in August 1985 so there was plenty of banter between the United and Liverpool elements in advance of the game. Chris Kinsey provided the most acute insight: 'The thing about the Charity Shield is that all the money goes to charity.' Thanks Chris. You can always tell those destined for the Senior Civil Service. It's an odd game the Charity Shield. Is it a trophy or not? I think the confusion is in the branding. If it was called the English Super Cup (with money to go to charity) and the shield was dispensed with then it would no doubt be a major honour. As it stands it's a major trophy if you win it and just a preseason friendly if you get battered. I watched the BBC highlights recently and how football has changed for the worse. Before the game Bob Paisley and Matt Busby did a lap of honour hand in hand on the back of a truck milking the applause of both sets of fans. Giants of both clubs.

The anti-football 1980s Tories with their overzealous police force and ID cards would have us believe that this would lead to some form of pitchside sectarian warfare. It was impeccably observed by the fans on both sides. Imagine Dalglish and Ferguson doing it now? In apparently more temperate times? Believe me, they would both be lynched before the halfway line. Then in injury time, with United two to the good and cruising, Robson is pulled down by Souness and denied a hat-trick. Robson implored the referee not to send off the Liverpool captain. Imagine the number of modern players brandishing mock red cards before the 250 million substitutes and nutritionists emerge from the respective bench to make matters worse? You can keep all that. My Sky Sports subscription was cancelled a long time ago.

So, we beat Liverpool with ease and two games in I had two medals. It's a bit like joining Barcelona in the summer and then three games into the new season having Super Cup and Spanish Super Cup winners' medals in your cabinet – you did nothing to get there but it will never show that in the book. Not bad this supporting United lark! I just remember wishing we could go to school on the Monday. Though I never knew it at the time, that post-victory Monday morning at school was the apotheosis of life – things could never get better and they didn't. I experienced this in the late springtime of the Brighton cup win, but this was Liverpool. It was different. It meant more. Their pain uplifted our pleasure to chemical heights and vice versa no doubt. True football fans are not only crypto sadomasochists; we are all addicts looking to recreate the first hit of that win over Liverpool or Bournemouth or Colchester. That is our whole raison d'être. Nothing more. Nothing less. No wonder we are all malcontents and misfits. No wonder we can't concentrate on our careers. No wonder we hate decorating and DIY. No wonder we hate garden parties and barbecues. No wonder we hate holiday brochures. No wonder we can't relate to women. No wonder we hate our in-laws. No wonder we hate the enthusiastic go-getter at work. No wonder we hate PowerPoint and Nintendo. No wonder we hate the non-footballing public. But like a true addict we will keep looking. One day we might find what we're looking for.

Back in the day the cup winners always trotted out a load of mince about 'mounting a serious title challenge next year, Brian'. Brian being Brian Moore of course. I loved Brian. John Motson was too loud and affected and it always annoyed me and my dad (OK my dad) that he pretended to trot out the most bizarre statistics from the top of his head ('I think Simon Stainrod started out at Orford Rovers in Warrington back in the day unless I'm very much mistaken, Trevor') as if we didn't know he had been locked underground with his football cards for a week beforehand. That sheepskin coat was the final nail in the coffin, not the first. The BBC coverage back then was awful. Five words: Jimmy Hill and Bob Wilson. I can remember Jimmy Hill inanely babbling on after we had lost to Argentina in 1986 and my dad, obviously pissed and pissed off anyway, said 'Shut your fucking chin up.' He hated Bob Wilson as well: he never trusted blokes in short sleeves and with eyes 'like piss holes in the snow'. Brian Moore was the Richie Benaud of football: a proper bloke. No bullshit. Anyway, of the mounting a title challenge next season it was imperative to add to the squad in the summer. The rhetoric was no different back then: 'We need strength in depth, Brian. Competition for places at 1 to 11. Especially as we'll be fighting on all fronts.' So, who did we acquire that summer? Charlie Nicholas? Steve McMahon? Mark Hateley? Paul Walsh? Ally McCoist? Andy Gray? John Barnes? Gary Lineker? Alan Smith? Lawrie Cunningham on a permanent? Arthur Graham was our sole addition to the squad that summer. A winger from Second Division Leeds United on the wrong side of 30 for £45,000.

Was this inertia Big Ron's fault? Something told me we needed an Ian Rush. A natural goalscorer with pace to burn. Thirty-plus a season guaranteed. But they do not grow toothbrush moustaches on trees. Ian Rush was at

Liverpool so out of bounds and if you look at the England international strikers of 1983 (Trevor Francis, Paul Mariner, Tony Woodcock) none of them were prolific. A punt on Gary Lineker would have been a huge gamble. To be fair to Big Ron he had brought Norman Whiteside through the season before as a 16-year-old and Mark Hughes was on the way too so you probably could not blame him for not paying a fortune for a more seasoned striker. We had Frank Stapleton too who was excellent. You can't praise managers for bringing through young players and then blame them a bit later for doing exactly that. He should have invested more in young players if anything. Peter Beardsley and David Platt? Did he see them play? Did he see them train? Did he speak to them? Did he know they were at the club? Did he fall out with the reserve team manager? Where was he at the time? From Crewe to Juventus. From Vancouver Whitecaps to Liverpool. That's one thing, but via Manchester United is criminally negligent. It's easy to be angry but you can't get them all right can you? Ronaldo (the Brazilian one) was released by Flamengo, Ruud Gullit shown the door by Arsenal at 19. It's a very long list: Platini, Zanetti, Diego Costa. It does happen. I was still very angry back then though, especially when Beardsley, who I loved for Newcastle and England, joined Liverpool. The silent rebellion? Around the autumn of 1987, I asked my female hairdresser (who was a proper dreamboat) for a Peter Beardsley haircut; I even brought her my *Shoot!* magazine to show her exactly what I meant!

The midfield was strong as well of course with Robson and Wilkins in central partnership; Arnold Mühren lent some class, quality and balance with that (wait for it ...)

'cultured left foot'. I never understood this blanket bias to left footers. When have you heard 'a cultured right foot'? And why the hell not? It was no better at school level either. Richard Gallion 'could open a tin of peas with that left foot' but never did, yet still remained in the side. He was as 'slow as a tax rebate' as well and in later years quite literally 'could not pass a pub'. It's not just football either: in cricket when have you heard of the 'elegant right hander having all the time in the world and making the game look easy'? Or a right-arm quick having the skill and variety of Wasim Akram?

Gordon McQueen and Kevin Moran were quality centre-backs and Mike Duxbury got up and down on the right flank before suddenly and inexplicably around 1986 he didn't. Arthur Albiston was 'Mr Consistency' at left-back and 'rarely had a bad game'. Roughly translated? He was an uncultured left-sided player who left the field drenched in sweat. So, 1 to 11 we were pretty decent, and this was before the isotonic days of the squad culture and rest and rotation and benches the size of Southend pier. Every First Division side would play its strongest side for a League Cup game at Rotherham and then again for whoever they faced that Saturday. That was just the way it was. And you were only allowed one substitute anyway. First-team squads were probably 13 or 14 at most and if there was an injury someone would be dragged in from the reserves. In 1981, Aston Villa used 14 players in their title-winning season. United in their last title-winning campaign of 2013 used 29 and 33 back in 2009. Villa played 42 games in 1981 compared to the 38 United played in 2009 and 2013. Big Ron had won the FA Cup in his second season and had built a decent side. He was doing well at this point.

So why then did my grandad, who visited us now and then for his tea after bowling at the Red Lion, once proclaim Atkinson to be a 'swine' when he barely said two words in life in general and didn't even like football that much? What inspired such ire from the man on the Clapham omnibus? Maybe it was the jewellery? The cream suits? The slip-on shoes? The perma-tan? The Arthur Scargill Shredded Wheat trim? A bit rich from a fella who wore three bad sweaters at once and managed to look like Bing Crosby and Val Doonican with a hint of Seve Ballesteros and the Michelin tyre man all at the same time. He preferred horse racing although he never bet. He also did not fear my fearsome dad. He would happily hog the Boxing Day TV with horse racing (the King George VI Chase), flick Embassy Mild fag ash on the snooker table and drop pint after pint of ale on the new carpet. Dad could not say a word. My sister and I loved it!

Act 3

Plug Me In

But for United fans Atkinson was far from a swine as the dank summer air of 1983 turned into the bloom of early autumnal colour. But what is it they say about lions in the autumn? Lambs in the spring … A Frank Stapleton header secured a 1-0 home win against Liverpool in late September. This was the second time in five weeks we had beaten Liverpool and they had failed to score in both games. I thought Kenny Dalglish and Ian Rush were supposed to be good? It was another excuse to get the ball out and see who was on the rugby club common. As the Liverpool fans sulked into their fizz bombs and Cannon and Ball, we were out in force; Tom Carter in full kit exhorting that 'Rush and Dalglish couldn't score in a brothel with a five-pound note'. I sang along but had no clue and while I didn't know what a bellend was either something told me not to ask when I got back home for crispy pancakes. We couldn't wait for Monday. Simon Stone never made it in. 'A heavy head cold.' Bollocks. How unconvincing! Another life lesson for sure. I resolved to make my Monday absences look much more genuine in the years ahead. Go from A to Z. Start with anaemia and end with zymotic diarrhoea and you won't go too far wrong …

Ron Inman from school was at the game he said but there again he said he taught Michael Jackson how to moonwalk. And he couldn't have moonwalked 20 miles back to Warrington in 15 minutes. Knowing Inny he probably hitched a ride on the wing of a Concorde. We might as well have waited for Inny to come back from Indiana to tell us the score because back then the information highway was treacherous terrain. If we were out messing around outside, which was the usual drill, then unless we found a radio, we had to wait for the final result in the *Manchester Pink* paper. The glass-infested, cinder track to Meachin's newsagent would puncture the most sturdy of Tomahawk or Grifter tyres, and even if it didn't there would always be someone on a BMX Super Burner to railroad you off the straight and narrow and get to the shop: David Lindop in fact. And Linny, who had just spent the preceding four hours kicking bruises of the deep crimson hue into my inner core around Warrington Rugby Union Club's rugby fields, would snaffle the last copy and then disappear into the ether, giving nothing away. How the hell did they get that paper to the shop so quickly? It was there at 5pm I swear! In full glory!

This was featured on *Match of the Day* that night and by now we had invested in a video recorder. A very big deal. The sandwich toaster was fine, but this was life-changing. Football could now be recorded and preserved, and I would not have to be dragged from bed four parts dead at 11pm every Saturday night. It was a Sharp video recorder too – just wish I had a United Sharp home shirt to go with it ... So that Sunday morning of 25 September I woke up and was ready to rewind and there was nothing to rewind. 'Dad's done it already,' I thought. All I got was *Russ Abbot's Madhouse*. Fantastic. Dad said it hadn't recorded, which I kind of worked out anyway, but the question, as always in life, is why? Were you brave enough to ask your dad why in 1983? Especially when two days later we were due to celebrate my sister's tenth birthday at McDonald's in town. We had never been before. We might never go. You did not jeopardise a McDonald's in 1983. Well over 30 years later I watched the highlights on YouTube. What struck me most was the intense pace of the game (according to popular football culture, players only started running circa 1992), the infernal din from the terraces and the throngs of supporters collapsing like dominoes down the Stretford End terracing whenever United threatened Bruce Grobbelaar's goal – a gloomy portent ...

But the autumnal frisson would never last. As rotten fermenting fruit dried up and fat wasps became colder and thinner our league form oscillated between inconsistent and unacceptable and our domestic cup campaigns imploded. A draw at home to Oxford United in the Milk Cup was followed by a defeat at the Manor Ground in the return leg. Oxford United and milk? Oxford United beating Manchester United over 270 minutes of football? After two replays? Oxford United of League Division Three? This was how fashionable football was in the dark final days of 1983 when unemployment topped three million, The Flying Pickets topped the charts and the IRA made us wonder if we would ever see Christmas. Robert Maxwell tried to buy United around the time, but chairman Martin Edwards rejected his bid of £10m. No bloody wonder! Robson himself was probably worth £3m. But was it as crazy an offer as it seemed? With zero TV money on the table, little in the way of sponsorship revenue or shirt sales and no overseas fan base, maybe it made sense. Especially given that the 27,459 hardy souls who attended the first replay at Old Trafford, paying little more than a quid to stand, could hardly have been expected to pay the wages of the big boys.

What if United had accepted the offer? You could see Maxwell asset-stripping the club of its best players and allowing the Stretford End to crumble into the cricket ground up the road. By the time the shit hit the fan of the Atlantic Ocean in 1991 we may have been in the Third Division and sold to a local businessman who owned two video hire shops and a Chinese chippy in Chorley. It may have been the Vauxhall Conference and Beazer Homes League by the time of Euro 1996 and the long journey upwards. Maybe that would have been for the better. A more interesting ride for the proper fan – a noble thing. I would have attended more games than I have done in the supervening 20 odd years. Maybe I should just stack it right now and throw my lot in with Gary Neville at Salford. The Bovril and meat pies from the snack shop look ace and that's what it should be all about.

What did I say earlier? Lions in the autumn, lambs in the spring? How about chokers in the winter? It certainly felt like that on 7 January 1984 when we went to Dean Court to take on Harry Redknapp's Third Division (that's

League Two to the digital generation) Bournemouth in the FA Cup third round. In case you have forgotten, we were the holders of the trophy. One thing: watch out for the clichés here; there are many. You may need to put your tickling sticks down. In fact, keep them out! This is the 1980s, the FA Cup, the seaside, Harry Redknapp is in the hotseat and United are in town. What do you expect other than rib-cracking, high-quality cliché analysis? Years later, when reminiscing to Jim White of the *Daily Telegraph* in an article dated 24 January 2014, Harry explained the emotions of the build-up: 'The whole coastline was buzzing.' No doubt there was a 'feel-good factor' as well. Surely a bit of David and Goliath?

Redknapp at this juncture was a young manager of just 36 years of age. He is the type of character who seems to have been born hangdog at 40 – all eyelids, paunch, knots and ligaments; so it's difficult to perceive him as a tracksuited innovator at the vanguard of anything remotely resembling footballing modernity. It's as incomprehensible as how Jamie can be even a distant relative, even 300 times removed. And many more things besides. Milton Graham was playing for Bournemouth that day. In a BBC Sport article by Nabil Hassan dated 23 January 2014 he remarked: 'It was just a dream to be playing against the best of the best.'

Ian Thompson, who also featured for The Cherries, added that he was 'honoured' at the prospect of being on the same park as Bryan Robson and Ray Wilkins and that 'The atmosphere in the town was incredible in the build-up to it, there was great excitement.' He also reserved some special praise for Sir Harry: 'I didn't notice a change in atmosphere in training. Harry kept our feet on the ground. He may not have believed we could beat them but he made us think we could and that was his great skill as a motivator.'

The night before the game, Sir Harry took the players to an Italian restaurant and the owner offered the Bournemouth keeper, Ian Leigh, a free pizza for life if he could keep a clean sheet. As legend would have it Sir Harry burst into the Bournemouth dressing room 20 minutes before kick-off claiming that the United boys were still in the directors' bar, watching the horse racing, bleary-eyed and placing bets.

'It probably wasn't true,' central defender Phil Brignull said in an article by Jack Pitt-Brooke in *The Independent* dated 11 December 2015, 'but it got us all going a little bit extra.'

Here is how we lined up that day:

1. Gary Bailey
2. Remi Moses
3. Arthur Albiston
4. Ray Wilkins
5. Graham Hogg
6. Mike Duxbury
7. Bryan Robson (captain)
8. Arnold Mühren
9. Frank Stapleton
10. Norman Whiteside
11. Arthur Graham

Substitute:
12. Lou Macari.

Five days before, we left Anfield with a point. Well, we left Dean Court with nothing. Other than a 2-0 defeat. This was the quintessential United of the 1980s – the sublime and the ridiculous. The Liverpool carrot means nothing unless you can repel the Bournemouth stick. That lesson took far too long to learn. Big Ron never learnt it.

'It wasn't a lucky result, given how we played,' continued Phil Brignull. 'They didn't have a shot on goal for 68 minutes. We dominated possession, and we shocked them.'

Sir Harry went much further in an article by Paul Wilson in *The Guardian* dated 11 December 2015: 'We'd been to Windsor & Eton in the previous round and got kicked to pieces,' he recalled. 'We got a draw and brought them back to ours knowing that whoever won the replay was going to play United. It was a proper old-fashioned Cup tie in the second round, a real tough game that we just scraped through. To be honest, we had less trouble with United than we did with Windsor & Eton.'

As to United players pissing about before the game, Redknapp maintained that this was not an apocryphal tale: 'Yeah, I saw a couple of them up in the lounge watching the 2.30 on the telly. I used that as a bit of a motivational thing. Mind, I thought they probably could have stayed and watched the 3.15 and still gone out and beaten us.'

And what about the keeper and his free pizza for life? Apparently, he had one or two margheritas on the house before the ownership of the restaurant changed hands. The new owner reneged on the offer: 'I had to,' explained Sir Harry. 'Nipper was already 5ft 10in and about 15st. He'd have eaten me out of business.'

Only in the FA Cup!

It's amazing that Bournemouth can beat United, Hereford can beat Newcastle, Colchester can beat Leeds and Plymouth Argyle can hold Liverpool. Is it the magic of the cup? If so, how can Leicester win the Premier League? Is something else at work? It's equally remarkable (according to all the anecdotal evidence) that every single goal scored by Jackie Milburn was at the Gallowgate End of St James' Park. Why then is he such a hero on Tyneside? He must have severely pissed off at least 50 per cent of the three billion crowd.

Truth be told we were struggling for goals in the spring of 1984. Stapleton and Whiteside were never prolific enough. In 1983/84, while Ian Rush netted 32 times in the league, Stapleton and Whiteside bagged just 23 between them. That was the difference between the two sides throughout the 1980s. As David Coleman said of Kevin Keegan when he put Liverpool ahead in the 1974 FA Cup Final, 'goals pay the rent and Keegan gets his share'. Stapleton and Whiteside did not get enough – hardly surprising as both played with their backs to goal. Too similar and too slow; one of them would have been fine with someone quick alongside them playing on the back defender making the most of the quality and vision of Robson and Wilkins. So, what do we do? We get Garth Crooks on loan – hardly a move designed to make Alan Hansen hit the Zolpidem and Drinking Chocolate. Two goals in seven games and then off to West Brom.

Before our seaside travails and struggles against cities renowned more for gowns and mortar boards than football we did progress to the European Cup Winners' Cup quarter-final. The previous round was in early November which was just as well as our 1984 league form was stodgier than a million marzipan fruits. For those of you under the age of 30 this now defunct European competition was played by the winners of each of the domestic cup competitions the previous season. Our route to the last eight could hardly be described as tortuous. It took only two ties; Dukla Prague and Spartak Varna were tiddlers and minnows, strangers to the Italian wine and Spanish meats of the European top table. Mind you, we only beat Dukla Prague on the away goals rule which was bollocks even then. We hear it all the time, don't we? Away goals count double. Away goals count double. It's like a bloody syndrome. But why do they? No good just stating the rule ad nauseam. Explain its logic please? Are the goals smaller for the visiting team in the away leg? Can they only play five and a half men? Do the home side have a two-goal start? Just what is it?

And we drew the mighty Barcelona in the quarters. It's an odd part of the football psyche. You always want the easy draw. So, what that means is you never want to tell your grandkids about the day you saw Maradona, Platini, Zidane or Messi captivate Old Trafford. You would much sooner draw Wrexham or Pécsi Munkás. And make no mistake this was Maradona's team. The first leg was a 2-0 reversal in Spain, and I can faintly recall from the crackling wireless Graeme Hogg scoring an own goal. There are a number of things unforgivable when you are eight and three quarters: own goals from a player on your side are pretty high on the list. Do you expect to find your mum's dandruff in the Sunday trifle?

Do you give a shit that she took reasonable care with the special formula on prescription from the chemist? Or that it is a condition that has blighted her entire life? And drained her social confidence and self-worth? No. It has ruined the fucking trifle – end of story. Do you care that Hogg was a teenager marking Maradona and his touch was probably the unavoidable ricochet of a bullet from a gun he didn't see? No. Hogg (o.g.): end of story. Harsh? Yes, but it's strict liability all the way at that age. I never forgave Graeme Hogg and when everyone else cried salt rivers of sympathy upon his omission from the cup final side a year later I was delighted. I had not forgotten. True football fans never do.

What chance a 3-0 win at home against the might of Maradona's men? The Barcelona juggernaut coached by the World Cup winner, César Luis Menotti. At school the day after the game in Barcelona all the Liverpool contingent were Maradona at break time (with a few of the more mordant ones Graeme Hogg) and I had to take it. They were riding high in the First Division, had defeated Benfica in the European Cup quarter-final (the proper European competition now known as the Champions League, not the comparative piece of tinfoil we were competing for) and were about to face Everton in the Milk Cup Final at Wembley. Look at where we were compared to them? Nowhere. We had to suck it up: all snot, blinkers, dirty collars and strangled tears. It hurt like the hell of cluster headaches without Chinese balm, but it made us mentally strong; not one manipulative girlfriend or Ming the Merciless boss could make us blink in the years ahead.

This is the United XI who took the field against Barcelona in the return leg against Barcelona on 21 March 1984:

1. Gary Bailey
2. Mike Duxbury
3. Arthur Albiston
4. Ray Wilkins
5. Kevin Moran
6. Graeme Hogg
7. Bryan Robson (captain)
8. Arnold Mühren
9. Frank Stapleton
10. Norman Whiteside
11. Remi Moses.

Save for Kevin Moran returning from injury (just for a change). this was exactly the same side who had lost at Bournemouth in the FA Cup back in January. Of course, Bournemouth did not bring a 2-0 lead into the game nor have the finest footballer that ever lived in their illustrious ranks. So, what happens? United 3-0, of course. Robson (2) and Stapleton. It's a mystery and yet it is not. Let's start with the mystery side: it defies logic and belief how the same defence which was beaten up, battered and bruised by Milton Graham and Ian Thompson can have Diego Maradona and Bernd Schuster in their arse pocket. Similarly, how can Stapleton and Whiteside rag doll defenders of the calibre of Alexanko and Moratalla on a night of tense electricity at Old Trafford and be totally inert on a quiet day out at the seaside? As mysteries go it's a bit like the failure of the Spira chocolate bar to dominate the world market given that EVERYONE in the north-west of England adored it when it was trialled between 1985 and 1989. Or why good-looking, quality women always seem to fall for football-hating, cap-wearing narcissists. Or why the only question anyone really wants to ask Paul McCartney is about John Lennon. But it is not a mystery: the Liverpool carrot can be the Barcelona carrot or the Real Madrid carrot. We would snaffle this with eager red eyes every day of the week and maybe expect some rabbit-friendly chocolate buttons for extra time. As for the Oxford and Bournemouth stick? Forget it. Would you expect a debonair young David Gower to graft to a 50 on a wet Championship Wednesday at Derby on a green seamer in front of one man and his cat? Exactly. It's the same thing.

We were still in the era when live games were essentially limited to cup finals, Home Internationals and World Cups but I am sure the radio snapped, crackled and popped a little bit louder that night as I huddled in the bunker of my freezing cold box room. I was allowed to stay up and watch the highlights as long as I promised not to tell Dad the score. He was no fool. He knew if we had lost: I'd be sulking until Easter Sunday; besides reluctant fathers never like taking their reluctant sons to bed when football is on unless they are not reluctant, in which case they are complete tossers. I can remember the energy of Robson, the comparative anonymity of Maradona, the chain-smoking of César Luis Menotti on the bench, and the incompetence bordering on fecklessness of the Barcelona goalkeeper. Oh, and Robson being chaired off like Apollo at the end. In his own words from an interview with manunited.com many years later:

> The first game hadn't gone to plan and I blamed myself because I'd had a couple of really good chances, so I just felt I owed the lads.
>
> The second leg went really well for us. We said we needed to try to get a goal in the first 20 minutes; we did that and went on.
>
> And the fans gave us so much energy. It was the best atmosphere I ever experienced at Old Trafford. A great win and great memories.
>
> My name was being sung and my back slapped till it hurt.
>
> But it was one of those nights you dream about and treasure for the rest of your life.

But why does history always have to be written by the winners? Winners can adapt the facts to suit the expedient of where they are now and what is expected of them. You know that revisionism we have all grown to hate? Big Norm set the record straight in a *Manchester Evening News* article by Tyrone Marshall dated 21 March 2020 (it seems he likes talking to everyone apart from me):

> Every time the question comes up about the best game I played in, for atmosphere it was the best game ever.
>
> I've played in World Cups and in cup finals but that night at Old Trafford it was electric. All those clichés such as the roof coming off, getting

goosebumps on the back of your neck, like having an extra man, they were all true that night.

I remember the likes of Paddy Crerand talking about the great European nights, I was wondering what to expect, I was only a kid and I hadn't experienced it yet.

Afterwards you realised what he meant, it truly was one of the great European nights at Old Trafford.

Barcelona had Diego Maradona and Bernd Schuster, they were the star players, most of the team were Spanish internationals.

The pressure was on, we had to go out and give it everything. People remember Bryan Robson having a brilliant game and scoring two goals, but the other thing they never remember is big Graeme Hogg marking Maradona out of the game. He hardly gets a mention.

Robbo got carried off at the end, it added to it being a memorable night.

History take note.

For every Bryan Robson there is a Graeme Hogg. It seems that the Barcelona apparatchiks took note of what they saw that night as well. Forget Menotti. Forget Schuster. Forget Maradona. Forget total football. Let's get Big Ron in. And the centre-half as well. What's his name? Graeme Hogg? Has he played for Scotland yet? What a great idea.

The man himself takes up the story in the 'Set Pieces' article by Andy Mitten dated 10 February 2015.

Shortly after we had knocked Barcelona out, the feelers started to come my way from Barcelona. My answer, discreetly passed along the grapevine, was simple. 'Sure, I'm ready to talk; just name the place.' I met the Catalan delegation at a London hotel. I confirmed that if everything regarding my United contract could be resolved with them, then I would be willing to move to Barcelona. To be frank, apart from the clearly exciting professional opportunity, it offered the perfect escape route from the domestic upheaval that was then brewing in my private life. I could have gone, closed a page and been spared so much hassle from the news boys as my first marriage broke up and my second, with Maggie, started. Just let me make the career jump, I thought at the time, and let me get the hell out of it. Oh, and my salary would have quadrupled.

During the initial discussion the only stumbling block was that Barça wanted me to join them on a two-year contract, which is the usual practice abroad; I countered that proposal with a demand for an extra year.

Seems an odd juxtaposition to me. But imagine if it did happen? No Johan Cruyff. No academy. No Iniesta. No Xavi. No Ronaldinho. No Messi. Big Norm in midfield, hacking away at all and sundry. Peter Barnes snoozing on the wing, claiming to the club president that a pre-siesta siesta was his contractual right. Tiki-taka pioneered by Graeme Hogg and Billy Garton. Relegation to the third tier? Presidential uproar? Turmoil in Catalonian sporting

INGLORY INGLORY MAN UNITED

politics as the majority turn to Real Madrid and Spanish rule for comfort. Jokes aside, Big Ron was definitely a viable choice. Terry Venables got the Barcelona job in the summer of 1984. He came from QPR and Crystal Palace before that. Hardly a great pedigree. Big Ron seemed, at the time at least, a much better candidate.

Meanwhile the last four of the Cup Winners' Cup beckoned but Juventus were a bridge too far in the semi-final. With the redoubtable attacking triumvirate of Platini, Boniek and Rossi, Juve were a far superior side to Barcelona, let alone a makeshift United outfit missing Bryan Robson in both legs. And it took an injury-time second-leg winner from Paolo Rossi in Turin to prevent extra time. A mighty good effort. Oh, but for Robson and his injuries! I mentioned earlier that we would have cleaned up with Ian Rush in our side and that's probably true, but Robson's regular injuries were just as damaging. In both 1982/83 and 1983/84 Robson played 33 of United's 42 league games; Graeme Souness featured in 37 for Liverpool in 1982/83 and 41 the following season. It's a significant difference. I am not a great fan of comparing different players; it's a pretty odious thing to do because you have to compare like with like. Robson and Souness were not similar players. Souness had better poise and vision; he could control games more; his passing had more imagination and variety; while Robson was quicker, stronger in the air, better box to box and scored more goals. It's a little like trying to compare Scholes and Gerrard. What cannot be argued is that they had a similar impact on the personality of the team and were equally as influential. We were not that far away from Liverpool – six points in 1983/84. Who knows what might have happened had Robson played a few more games?

After the Juventus defeat, our 1983/84 domestic campaign gently meandered towards fourth place and the security of a UEFA Cup spot. Minds turned to Majorca and Corfu. No sunbeds or beers on the beach for Liverpool unfortunately. Having triumphed domestically in both the league and League Cup they travelled to the eternal city to take on AS Roma in the European Cup Final. A European Cup Final in your own stadium? In front of your own fans? What more did they want? Jam on it? Was it unfair? Yes, of course, but not, of course, on this occasion. It was bloody hilarious! Christians to the lions? Fat chance. Liverpool won on penalties. If I had a pound over the years for every time some lazy journalist had called penalties a 'lottery' I would have 17 pounds by now. It is compelling viewing and what greater test of skill and character than having to step up under shit-hot crucible pressure after 120 minutes of muscle-knotting graft. It is only a lottery when Liverpool win it, like it was in Rome in 1984 and again in Istanbul many years later.

Act 4

I'd Have You Anytime

What is it about summer in the 1980s that breathed hope eternal? Was it the balmy languid days of freshly cut grass, leisurely barbecues, lemon squash and Boris Becker? The rhythm of David Gower's cover drive set against the soundtrack of Brian Johnston's cakes and comedy? In part I guess but maybe more towards the end of the 1980s when I knew a cover drive was not desecrating my sister's *Jackie* magazine with my school compass. As an eight-and-three-quarter-year-old in August 1984 it was more to do with the imminent arrival of the League Ladders in the *Shoot!* magazine. You were either *Shoot!* or *Match Weekly*. I'd have liked both, but my dad was so tight that his hearing aid had a solar-panelled battery. *Shoot!* was better – fantastic columnists like Bryan Robson, Graeme Souness, Ian Rush, Steve Archibald. And I also remember Greavsie's postbag – star letter a tenner, any other published a fiver. I wrote to Jimmy a hundred times without fruit; mind you, one of them circa 1989 was lamenting that United signed Gary Pallister rather than Glenn Hysén! What the hell do I know? PS Favourite joke of United fans around 1991? What have Glenn Hysén and Saddam Hussein got in common? They are both shit in the air.

Teletext improved things a bit towards the mid-1980s for real-time football gossip and banter. I got an A in Information Technology some years later but it was exam only: you probably got docked marks if you went near a computer, and if you even breathed over the shift button you felt that you had just dropped the bomb. Mr Wilson at our school certainly defended the few computers we had with a cold-war Scouse militant zeal. So, the first question in my GCSE Information Technology exam? 'What is the difference between Ceefax and Oracle?' Don't worry: we were all well drilled. Ceefax was the C in BBC which meant that the Oracle was ITV's version. 'Who are you, the oracle?' they would ask when I would showreel through each FA Cup winner since 1961 and name each scorer on the winning and losing sides. 'No. I'm the Ceefax,' I would reply. No wonder I'm shit at IT and girls hate me.

Teletext aside, *Shoot!* was still considered a reliable and up-to-date source. I recall once in April 1989 Ian Rush appeared on the cover adorned in a blue NEC Everton shirt. The inside pages documented Rushie's boyhood affiliation, his belief in the post-Kendall paradigm and while Evertonians and United fans rejoiced, Liverpool fans cried a new River Mersey, all salty, bitter and red. We ALL believed it. A medley of Puch Prima 12 bikes grinded their way to the rugby playing fields to discuss the bombshell. Then on the last page the joke was unveiled: edition date: 1 April 1989. Then it was back home to the dice football: the only way you could make sure that United won the double. Once that was achieved maybe there was time for a bit of *Football Manager* on the ZX81 if you had ten years to wait for it to load from the cassette. Nowadays, real time is thrice-hourly updates on irrelevant bullshit: who cares how Wayne Routledge's slight thigh strain is responding to the RICE protocol? Or the ongoing disclosure battle in the ex-Cowdenbeath manager's legal battle for compensation?

Shoot! also had fantastic free gifts. We got a free Striper bar in September 1983, much to my sugar-starved sister's chagrin. No, she got nothing, not even a centimetre. And then just before the Charity Shield curtain raiser the League Ladders came out. The ladders were cardboard strips with inch-long insertions for each position and came with cut-out tabs corresponding to each team. What unbridled joy to put United top of the First Division and Liverpool bottom of the Fourth. Back then there was no relegation to the non-league and no promotion from it. All the bottom club in the Fourth Division would have to do was to apply for re-election which would pretty much be automatically granted. Pretty bloody unfair if you ask me. I'd use my dad's phone he brought home from work to deal with the re-election process. Needless to say, Liverpool's application for re-election was never granted.

The summer was always an exciting time for United fans. New players were marketed as the Holy Grail: men of steel and minerals, destined to turn us from contenders into title winners. Anyone who once drifted wide in the Under 10s preseason five-a-side was the new Georgie Best; any central midfield player who could hoof the heavy ball a bit was the new Bobby Charlton; and anyone who once scored a brace for Molde's youth team in Norway was the new Denis Law. Players in the 1980s had arrived with big reputations in the past and not delivered. No doubt they were ready for the challenge ahead: exercise books backed with United wallpaper, pencils sharpened, PE kit meticulously labelled; however, well before October half-term the exercise books were stained with last-minute breakfast marmite; the pencils dulled, stunted, broken or stolen; and PE kit was left gathering mushrooms and mucor in the lost property bin. Garry Birtles springs to mind.

But, of course, 1984 was to be different. Ray Wilkins had been sold to AC Milan and we had bought an exciting triumvirate of attacking talent in Jesper Olsen, Gordon Strachan and Alan Brazil. It was like Best, Law and Charlton really. Except that Olsen was also dubbed as the most exciting thing since Danish bacon and Johan Cruyff, so no pressure there. Although he weighed about 3st piss-wet through no doubt, some plank in the media called him 'The Great Dane'. Every Dane who leaves the airport in Copenhagen is 'The Great Dane' regardless of how shit they actually are. Strachan was a proven winner with Aberdeen and made complete sense. Brazil was an odd one. We needed pace up front and according to my dad 'he had seen milk turn quicker'. Whatever that meant. However, three goals in 19 games for Spurs in an injury-ravaged campaign the season before needed no explanation. But what was just as important as what we had gained was what Liverpool had lost: Souness to Sampdoria. Rush would miss the first couple of months of the season with injury. Dalglish was now 33 years of age as well. Opportunity knocked.

Gordon Strachan once said that shortly after his arrival at Old Trafford during preseason training the first-team squad were playing a five-a-side as chaotic and discordant as any of those 28-a-side twilight variants we played. Big Ron showed up with a valise case which seemed to show some degree of gravitas. Strachan fully expected him to unfurl a dossier about Watford (our opponents on opening day), a debrief about Luther Blissett and John Barnes's movement, a Subbuteo pitch going through our own tactics, a flip chart, felt-tip pens, highlighters, a pointer stick or any such adjunct to tactical analysis. This was, after all, Manchester United; he was also, of course, accustomed to the meticulous preparation of Alex Ferguson and Archie Knox at Aberdeen. Instead, Big Ron produced a portable fold-up 'deck' chair, a radio, sun cream, assorted fruits, cheeses and champagne; he then de-shirted and proceeded to soak up the rays. I just hope the inevitable grunts and groans of the five-a-side did not disrupt his enjoyment of John McEnroe's topspin, down-the-line forehand or Viv Richards's insouciant flick through midwicket: it wasn't like there was any work to do.

The first Old Trafford game I went to was the Watford game. Saturday, 25 August 1984. It was my mate's birthday and his dad was taking us, so my own dad had no choice in the matter; for the record he still hadn't taken me to Old Trafford (nor did he seem likely to given his sky-blue proclivities and well-known parsimony), nor bought me a United shirt. The latter was unforgiveable. My birthday had just passed and as United changed strips for the new campaign the old shirts were selling for a couple of quid. Suffice to say I didn't get one and I was not best pleased at the Superman T-shirt I thought might (just might) be the old home strip (or even the away). Just my luck it was a boiling hot day so my mum decided it would be 'a great idea if I wore the Superman shirt Nan bought me'. Dad agreed and did not hide his amusement. 'What's so funny?' asked Mum. So, the day ahead which should have been a joyous occasion saw me pissed off before I had even found my peg jeans and Gola trainers. The birthday boy Ellis Chapman hardly helped matters. There he was resplendent in the **new** home strip. 'Are you going in that T-shirt, Jamie?' Fuck off mate. It actually got worse because his dad had booked tickets in the Stretford End which was standing. Maybe he didn't know much about football or United or the fact that his son and I were knee-high to Jesper Olsen. Maybe he left the orange boxes in his Datsun Sunny? Or perhaps he was just a dick? Anyway, I couldn't see a bloody thing and I lost count of the number of times I was asked 'Is it a bird, is it a plane ...' I started to hate United fans. When Watford equalised right at the end, I was almost pleased as it shut these tossers up.

It was a strange season of top-heavy draws. In fact, we drew each of our first four games. Why does Big Ron never take his dog out for a walk? Because he can't hold the lead. It wasn't until 8 September that we registered a victory (5-0 against Newcastle at home) and while we were still undefeated after eight games going into October, we had only won three of them. It did not take long for the draws to turn into defeats. I can remember us playing Everton at the back end of October. Big Ron in the lead-up was promoting his book entitled *United to Win*. Bit rich given all the draws. Well, perhaps not after a 5-0 win. To

Everton. Given their FA Cup win the previous May lots of blues were crawling out of the woodwork, so we now had both the blue and red of Merseyside to worry about on the playground Monday morning. It wasn't easy being me in October 1984. Something told me this was going to be another campaign based around the cups. A fight on three fronts: League Cup, FA Cup and UEFA Cup. Has anyone ever done this treble before? Four days after the massacre at Goodison Park, Everton beat us again, this time in the League Cup and on our own dung heap. I was out trick or treating that night but my tears had nothing to do with the scary monsters (we all knew it was Lee Smith putting the bangers in our parka hoods), the chippy not accepting halfpennies or the door-slamming alcoholics. But we recover quickly from first-degree burns and starvation rations when we are kids. What about a cup double then? Home and abroad? Not for the first time Big Ron would be pleading mitigation of this sort at the late autumn board meeting.

Football and TV? What do you think? A marriage made in heaven or in Albert Square? The first league game screened live by ITV was Spurs v Forest in October 1983. The BBC followed suit soon after with United v Spurs on a Friday night. I think the clubs were suspicious to begin with. I'm sure they got very little by way of TV money after the Football League had taken its cut and they were probably worried that this would impact on attendances; indeed the 33,616 who turned up at Old Trafford for the United v Spurs game in December 1983 probably bore this out. This was well down on the 43,664 who saw the previous Saturday home game against Everton two weeks or so earlier. The experiment continued: I recall specifically a Friday night live televised game against Arsenal at Old Trafford played in driving, unrelenting rain. That day (Friday, 2 November 1984) we moved house so I remember it well – the early start, the juggernaut removal van, the Wrigley's Spearmint Gum, the hairy arses, the endless brews, the badly packed tea chests, the arguing, the bad moods, the fish and chips. Dad did not pay for the latter; a lovely family friend did. We got a fish each as well (not half to share) and curry sauce. And a can of cream soda each (not to share). Fish and chips? In November? I could barely believe it. Halley's Comet was spotted in Warrington that night, I think. If not, there was definitely a guild fair in Preston. It's a shame we only moved once.

The TV coverage was definitely odd, but any new relationship is. Your new girlfriend's stroganoff is always rank, but you don't judge it – you fire it into the bowl or the dog. She sits on your settee and not hers. She gets the wrong biscuits. She leaves the teabag in for two seconds rather than 25 minutes. You have to give it time. Eventually when she settles down and begins to hate you, she will abandon the stroganoff and it will be pie and chips in the oven; everyone is happy then. In fact, some features of Friday night football were quite interesting. There was the short-lived experiment of half-time interviews with players and managers – this generally consisted of Bryan Robson stating, 'We're doing well, Tony, but there's still 45 minutes to go.' This particular half-time Big Ron vented his spleen to Tony Gubba: 'Our players need to learn how to defend.' True, Gary Bailey could have had a cup of tea and bara brith and still stopped Tony Woodcock's dribbler which put Arsenal in front just before the break but how can you complain about bad defending when Graeme Hogg is in the team? And you picked him? Maybe the cameras should have been allowed into the dressing room as well? Or the referee's room? There was definitely something in the half-time idea if it was followed through properly and carefully expanded.

'What's a wanker, Dad?' I asked as the Stretford End roared its disdain at Champagne Charlie Nicholas in the second half. For once, perhaps for the first time even, he was silent – of course the moments of rare silence both then and later were moments when words and explanation were actually needed. But football is football – a pointless but wonderfully rich and unpredictable diversion. Don Howe on the Arsenal bench adorned a blue and red windcheater Nike cagoule which was soon to become de rigueur on primary school playgrounds; well, ours anyway. Don Howe the arbiter of fashion and style for a generation? Perhaps not, but only through football and football fashion culture could it be cool in any way to resemble him. I loved his enthusiasm for the game too: in the early 90s when Channel 4 somehow acquired rights to live Serie A games he was one of the regular summarisers. He could never get the name Sampdoria right: it was always Samapadoria, even after Des Walker joined. He would also tell Peter Brackley how he had been 'waiting for this game all week'. Why? Did he not know what time it started? Still he was bloody miles better than Paul Elliott and Luther Blissett.

So why did live Friday night football never take off? Can we blame Don Howe for this? Maybe the public had been waiting for the game all week and had simply grown bored by early Friday evening? It's tempting to say that blokes told their wives they were going to the game, then just went to the pub and bought a few more beers and pork scratchings to watch the game in comfort. This would not show a tick in the attendance at the game box or in the TV figures, but it doesn't mean that people were against it. Maybe the more eager to please husbands did stay at home but in between the grouting and the squeaky floorboards and Coronation Street the football didn't get a look-in. Those who did watch it unashamedly with a beer and a fag would probably have been divorced by March 1985. Friday nights might have been date nights: you know, leave the kids with people you have never seen in your life and hope that the offer of a settee and a free cheese roll will persuade Terry and Sandra to keep their hands to themselves. Maybe Monday to Friday family life could only sustain *A Question of Sport* on a Tuesday night with a bit of *Sportsnight* thrown in now and then? Whatever way you look at it the clubs did suffer; and they were probably right to demand a larger slice of the suet pudding TV rations on offer back then.

No European games were shown live. Not even our barnstorming UEFA double header with Dundee United. Back then top Scottish sides were a good match for the top English sides. The previous season Dundee United reached the semi-final of the European Cup; they won the home leg against Roma 2-0 only to lose 3-0 in Rome in the return fixture. Most top English sides had a quality Scottish player or three in their ranks: we had Albiston, McQueen and Strachan; Liverpool had Hansen, Dalglish and Nicol; Spurs had Archibald; Arsenal had Charlie

Nicholas. I cannot remember the last time an English side (or any other side for that matter) spent top brass on a quality Scottish player. What are the kids doing up there? So, Dundee United was a tough challenge not made easier by a 2-2 draw at Old Trafford in the first leg. How I craved to watch the return at Tannadice Park. Tom Carter and I asked his dad, who was a policeman, whether he would take us. He said no. I thought all policemen were helpful back then. The Saturday before, we walked to Warrington Central Station in town to enquire how much a half return to Dundee was. We would worry about tickets when we got there. And the bollocking when we got back. We were told it was 20 quid for the pair of us. We prized open our NatWest Saver pigs and liberated about £1.73. We might as well have walked to Scotland.

What made it worse was that midweek sports TV was very limited. *Sportsnight* and *Midweek Sports Special* was OK from time to time but generally it was on too late and you were not allowed to stand up and watch. Amidst the hurly-burly of last-ditch homework and soggy cornflakes there was not enough time to watch all of it in the morning before school. You'd get to the point ten minutes into the first half when Arthur Albiston was taking a throw-in, then you'd get the final call from Dad (the one that meant business); half an hour later everyone at school had reconstructed each passage of play so you'd sooner watch *He-Man* or *The Flumps* when you got back home. *A Question of Sport* never did it for me until Ian Botham took over from Emlyn Hughes. David Coleman and Emlyn Hughes have to be the unfunniest combination since Mickey Rooney teamed up with Judy Garland. Every bloody week the same joke. The second round of the picture board Emlyn would ask for number 6 when it had already been opened and answered in the first round. Every sodding week! He was no better on *Sporting Triangles* which was shit as well. Even with Beefy though I could never totally enjoy the show if a United player appeared: I was too scared he would get an easy football question wrong or wear a shit jumper out of C&A. I would not hear the end of it the next day; it's still the same now in law but they call it vicarious liability.

But this time it would be different. The radio I decided was to blame. If I got to sleep earlier, I could nip downstairs and watch the full highlights without knowing the score. When Arnold Mühren put us 3-2 up with ten minutes or so remaining with a horribly deflected shot it was all I could do to contain my excitement. I surreptitiously went upstairs to collect my balloon so I could reconstruct the strike using the living room door frame as a goal. For once I would be well prepared for school the next day. And for the weekend. My mate's dad worked for British Aluminium and they held a Christmas party each year for the kids and their friends. So in between the jelly and the cheese and pineapple on sticks and the blindfolds and the parcels I was able to talk people through the goals. Santa just stuck to the script; I think he was a Liverpool fan. Warrington was a town that had several big employers back in the day (Greenall's Brewery where Dad worked and Tetley Walker's Brewery which employed my uncle) and each of them put on a great Christmas event for the kids. I can remember many a coach trip to a circus or a panto and a gargantuan bag of sweets. Now we just have law firms and call centres who sack people who have not already quit. Really sad. These were the best days, you know.

Then the quarter-final draw pitted us against the might of Videoton. We always judged teams back then by how shit the name sounded. When a couple of years later I had turned to Under 11 we assumed, using the same logic, that Lockingstump Eagles must be rubbing rags. We didn't kick a bloody kick. That Band Aid Christmas of 1984 saw us play Stoke City away on Boxing Day. They had a keeper called Barry Siddall who I saw on the Panini stickers. I concluded on the basis of his bald pate and full beard that he must be the worse stopper ever. OK, it wasn't just that: Stoke were rooted to the bottom of the First Division and I had seen Siddall make a few errors on the TV, but you get the point. We lost that day 2-1. I lost the plot. Dad, no doubt fortified with the copious vats of free Yuletide ale he took from work, took the piss more than normal. I dunked a Trio in his pint pot and jabbed him in the mouth. To be fair, I had only just seen *Rocky I*, *II* and *III* so it was a kind of rite of passage. Only the season of goodwill and my grandad's reassuring presence ensured I saw 1985 and kept a fulminating Ivan Drago away from Warrington WA4. Of course, in time-honoured United tradition we demolished Chelsea at Stamford Bridge 48 hours later and I was happy again. Had I learnt any lesson? Not a chance. Videoton of Hungary would be an unspoiled walk in the park.

The UEFA Cup was an odd one. Only the winners of the European leagues would qualify for the European Cup. So why didn't they call it the Champions League? The UEFA Cup would be contested by teams who had finished second, third and fourth in the major European leagues and maybe second or third in countries like Romania or Hungary. Given that most European teams did not and do not care much for the domestic cup competitions (read Copa del Rey and Coppa Italia) the UEFA Cup was probably stronger than the Cup Winners' Cup. So, the 1984/85 UEFA Cup saw very strong Real Madrid and Roma sides who had been pipped for the league title the previous year. Now the runners-up and second and third and fourth are all in the Champions League. Make sense? No, it doesn't, does it? Anyway, we beat Videoton at home but by a narrow 1-0 margin. Around this time, I began to absorb some of the bullshit vernacular around European ties, but I understood none of it. So, while we had won, it was apparently a bad result? But it was still a good result although technically a bad result as we had not conceded an away goal. Confused? I still am. Try studying EU law as I had to.

The second leg in Hungary kicked off around the same time I arrived home from school on the afternoon of Wednesday, 20 March 1985. In a gift from the gods Dad had purchased a new Hitachi TV the weekend before. I did think Dad's squash partner had wrapped his racket round his head causing organic brain damage. Dad and a new TV? And Teletext as well? He'd surely have to pay extra for that. But he received his new company car around the same time, and we were now in a better area of town so maybe he was becoming a bit more that way inclined. There was more to it now you see. The snooker table alone would not quite cut the Harrods mustard in 1985. You had posher neighbours and needed visitors to match. It was the era of the chilli and barn dance brigade: a mahogany world of dinner parties, place mats and orchard gold. Conversing over red wine with the directors of companies going nowhere fast.

Showing off with After Eight mints and Viennetta. 'Pass me the stilton please, Clive.' 'Any port to go with it, Irene?' Lashings of real lemonade passed over the fence on those sultry summer days. He was creosoting the railings and building a birdbath by the summer. He was school governor selling raffle tickets by October. There was talk of round-table hustings in early 1986. Jesus Christ. Bollocks to all that.

I can still remember it was page 140 on Ceefax for sport. If you found me that Hitachi remote now, I could navigate it blindfold. It was welded to my hand between 1985 and 1993; I could land Concorde with it at one point. So, I settled into Ceefax and I would have alternated between page 141 (which would have all the scores) and page 142 which would have the score flash update system. It was propitious that this was a Wednesday; Tuesday or Friday would have meant competition from *Grange Hill* which I loved as well. Zammo McGuire or United. Jesus! That's a tough one.

Dad was a pain in the arse with the Teletext. At crucial points in games played around this time of day he would ring to ask me to check the share price of Amstrad or orange juice or some other piece of shit his new Tory mates had moved him towards. That soon stopped after Black Monday and BP: making money for Maggie was not quite as easy as it seemed. At some point the score flash registered VIDEOTON 1 MAN UNITED 0 and the remote got the first of many dints off the fireplace hearth.

No matter how much my fingers bled it was still 1-0 to Videoton and we headed to penalties.

The score flash system told the story of the shoot-out:

VIDEOTON 1 MAN UNITED 0
VIDEOTON 1 MAN UNITED 1
VIDEOTON 2 MAN UNITED 1
VIDEOTON 2 MAN UNITED 2
VIDEOTON 3 MAN UNITED 2
VIDEOTON 3 MAN UNITED 2 (MISS – STAPLETON MAN UNITED)
VIDEOTON 4 MAN UNITED 2
VIDEOTON 4 MAN UNITED 3
VIDEOTON 4 MAN UNITED 3 (MISS – GOMORI VIDEOTON)
VIDEOTON 4 MAN UNITED 4
VIDEOTON 5 MAN UNITED 4
VIDEOTON 5 MAN UNITED 4 (MISS – ALBISTON MAN UNITED)
VIDEOTON WIN.

This was my first experience of technology. No wonder I hate it so much. To any ex-bosses out there? You can blame Arthur Albiston for all those links that never worked and the Zoom meetings I never attended, not to mention the scrag endnotes which I was told ought to be in a PowerPoint or a Spreadsheet. You know what? Despite what I said I never even fucking tried either! If we had have won that day, I'd now be a master programmer at IBM. Thank God we did bloody lose! Arthur Albiston saved my soul. Not that night he didn't. This was the first time

I ever tore down the United posters in my room with the rage of molten tears burning my face and scarring my soul. Not the last. Not by a long shot.

Act 5

Out of the Blue

Plus ça change, plus c'est la même chose, as I learnt in the Dordogne or A level French. In other words, it was now early April and as usual for United it was the FA Cup or bust. Oh, and the small matter of Liverpool in the semi-final. Two weeks before, we beat them in the league at Anfield courtesy of a Frank Stapleton header. I felt this was a bad omen; if we won when it mattered less (as we were out of contention in the league yet again) then Videoton's Law suggested that we would choke when it mattered the most. I can remember arriving back from playing a club match that afternoon with the game at Anfield about an hour in and delicately poised at 0-0. Dad was not happy when the match had not recorded; he liked to watch it from the beginning and he was very pleased he had avoided the radio waves and the touchline murmurings with his Bruce Springsteen 'Born in the USA' headphones.

My sister got a bollocking for messing with the tape. Why would she do that though? It seems very unlikely she would risk a volley to record *Supergran*? He knew it was his fault, but he would never admit it. After my sister got despatched to clean Jasper the rabbit's cage, I got the blame for the afternoon fixture. Like I planned it? Like I was the league secretary? He hated afternoon fixtures ('They make a complete bollocks of the whole bloody day.') and Stapleton's winner hardly improved his mood. Mum had some shelves to be put up in extra time as well. Poor Dad. His work life may have been good but maybe his home life was not? But if you want to join the middle classes, Kenneth? We all know that feeling in the end. The unforgiving foe of opportunity cost. What did I want? Dead easy. To win the FA Cup.

Such philosophical questions were not on the agenda on semi-final day, but Dad still had chores to do: paint the inside window frames, sills and skirting boards.

Simon Stone, my Liverpool mate, was round: I have to take the credit for some judicious planning here. With a live and independent corroborative witness, Dad wouldn't murder me if I put my hand in the paint (which of course I did three or four times despite his 127 warnings) and, more importantly, I could savage Stoney if we won and take his best if we lost! Monday was therefore sorted either way. You can always tell those destined to be distinguished lawyers. Ron Atkinson set the tone in an interview with ITV's Brian Moore when he said: 'This weekend will either be the best of the season or the worst for many a long year.' He was getting better at this media lark.

We lined up as follows at Goodison Park on the afternoon of Saturday, 13 April 1985:

1. Gary Bailey
2. John Gidman
3. Arthur Albiston
4. Norman Whiteside
5. Paul McGrath
6. Graeme Hogg
7. Bryan Robson (captain)
8. Gordon Strachan
9. Mark Hughes
10. Frank Stapleton
11. Jesper Olsen.

Quite a few changes from the line-up which had beaten Liverpool in the Charity Shield at Wembley 18 months or so earlier. Whiteside had been converted into a midfield player (what did I say about a lack of pace?) and Mark Hughes (not known for his pace either) operated up top with Frank Stapleton (no pace either). Paul McGrath, who would become imperious for club and country when health allowed, was now a mainstay at centre-back (although he was superb in midfield too) and Olsen and Strachan were the wide men. Stoney arrived around 12pm. He enjoyed Mum's dinner (not lunch back then) of cheese and TUC crackers with Branston pickle and a cup of soup as much as I enjoyed smashing him at Pac-Man, Space Invaders and River Raid; Christmas 1984 saw the addition of an Atari to the middle-class prefab kit. Then it was on to the serious business. It was radio commentary we opted for that day. I got the distinct feeling that we were bossing it. Stoney knew as much about the game as I did and was sangfroid about perceived domination. 'It only takes a second to score a goal and we have Ian Rush.' What can you say to that?

Half-time ticked over towards 70 minutes in. A corner on the left swung in by Strachan, flicked on by Hogg and smashed home by Robson in typical style. Stoney locked himself in the bathroom. I touched Dad's wet paint in unbridled joy and didn't give a single shit. Who cares about a bit of paint when you are off to Wembley? Four minutes left and it was role reversal time. Ronnie Whelan played a one-two with Phil Neal on the edge of our box and curled a delightful right-foot shot tantalisingly past Bailey's outstretched hand. Stoney may have put his hand in the paint too; I certainly blamed him when he went home later on. We shook paint-drenched hands before extra time. Eight minutes in and Stapleton's soft daisy-cutter from outside of the box inexplicably beat Grobbelaar and found the net. It was deflected, of course, as was Robson's, but we don't talk about that. There was no celebration this time. We had to see the game out. Extra time of extra time and the linesman flags for offside against Liverpool. That's it surely? I know it. A lachrymose Stoney knows it. But the referee didn't see the flag. Play continues and a deep cross from Dalglish is headed towards goal by Rush. Bailey can only parry it towards the onrushing Paul Walsh who bundles it over the line. Stoney does a lap of honour. I tell him to 'fuck off and go home'. My planning for Monday did not legislate for a bloody draw. We had to do it at Maine Road again on the Wednesday night.

We had surely lost our chance. I read all the papers now and they said as much. Liverpool couldn't play as badly again if they tried. Joe Fagan commented after the match (as reproduced in a *Guardian* article by Steven Pye dated 12 April 2013): 'We didn't really deserve what we got. When they went 2-1 ahead in the first half of extra time, I felt we could all go home, so I am very thankful we have got another crack at it.'

The Maine Road replay started badly, and we were one down at half-time. Pardon my French but Stoney was a fucking cheeky bastard. At half-time the phone rang. My sister answered: 'It's for you, nob. Your dickhead mate.' I knew who it was. I didn't need to hear the '1-0 1-0 1-0' chorus. A minute after half-time it was 1-1 – a 25-yard piledriver from Robson after a typical marauding run through the heart of midfield. Just short of the hour and an adroit through ball from Strachan sent away Hughes to place a right-foot shot beyond Grobbelaar. There was a huge hint of offside about it. I reached for the phone to return the favour to Stoney. Unfortunately, they were noisier than a Wall Street trading floor back then: 'You can use that bloody phone when you pay the bloody bill.' Oh well, revenge is best served cold in the playground on Thursday morning. And it was. We hung on to win 2-1.

It was Robson Rovers again. Hindsight 20 or more years later sometimes removes the emotion of the moment which is what sport is all about. This is the conversation Robson had with Elton Welsby of ITV Sport in the tunnel at Maine Road straight after the final whistle:

> Elton: Bryan. A marvellous moment for you?
> Robson: Yeah it is, Elton, because Liverpool are the team to beat. They've done it for years and years. And they never give you a minute's peace

when you play against them so it's a great result for the boys.

Elton: What was said at half-time when you were 1-0 down?

Robson: We were reminding ourselves of when we came back against Arsenal. We've done it once so there's no reason we can't do it again.

Elton: Quite a timely goal you scored?

Robson: It was lovely to see it go in cos since I've come back from injury my shooting has not been very good at all. So, it was lovely to see that one fly in.

Elton: Any doubt after Mark Hughes put you 2-1 ahead that Liverpool might come back again?

Robson: There were doubts as sometimes things come in threes. Thankfully it didn't.

Elton: What about the magnificent scenes at the end? That must have warmed every United player and supporter?

Robson: They're great supporters. They've turned out in fantastic numbers again tonight. And they stick by the team whether we're winning or losing so they're great fans.

Elton: I know emotions are running very high at the moment but have you had time to think about the FA Cup Final against Everton and what sort of match that will be?

Robson: No, not really. It's a long way off and we've got a few league games to go before that. We have to make sure if we don't win the championship we qualify for Europe.

Elton: One or two celebrations tonight?
Robson: (smiling) I think so.

Pure gold! What a lovely interview! Robson an absolute legend but a normal bloke without edge or agenda enjoying talking openly to a reporter he clearly likes. They probably had a beer together just after. Not like the media-trained lot of today who spit indifference with each monosyllable towards the hand that feeds them diamonds for breakfast. Whatever happened to Elton Welsby by the way? He was all over everything at ITV, then he just vanished. First into crown green bowls and then into thin air. A bit like the SDP. I hope he's OK. Robson was always as gracious in defeat as in victory, unlike Alan Hansen who (in comments reproduced in an ESPN article entitled 'A rivalry in deepest red' by Robin Hackett dated 3 March 2011) remarked that 'The second goal was ten yards offside.' Piss off Alan: you've won enough to know a bit about luck so don't complain when one goes the other way. Mind you, even Big Ron said it was 'marginal'. Who cares anyway? It's in the book and if it rankles with them still then all the better. And forget all this nonsense about the quality of the game back then. Rob Smyth, in his *Guardian* article entitled 'The Joy of Six' dated 15 April 2011, remarked upon both semi-finals: 'The first game was a minor classic, finishing 2-2, and the second match was even better. This was football as nature intended, a relentlessly attacking slugfest played by proper men in front of proper men, in an atmosphere that, 26 years on, effortlessly shivers the spine.' Hear hear! You can keep your La Liga. And your Serie A. With all your easy fixtures and pretentious style over substance possession. Give me passion, guts and thunder any day of the week. As long as we win, of course.

I think the excitement of beating Liverpool got to me, even 35 years later! It was Everton we would face in the final on Saturday, 18 May 1985. They won the First Division title for the first time in 15 years that season, 13 points clear of Liverpool in second place. We, as usual, were fourth; we would have been great in the present day when finishing fourth seems more important than winning the bloody thing. There'll be a trophy for it soon. Everton had also triumphed in the Cup Winners' Cup three days earlier when they defeated Rapid Vienna in Rotterdam. They were a fine side: in any era, other than immediately post-Heysel, they would have received more critical acclaim and possibly the biggest European prize. Neville Southall was indubitably the best keeper in the world in 1985. Miles better than Peter Shilton or Jean-Marie Pfaff. Kevin Ratcliffe had a touch of Baresi about him: a brilliant sweeper with pace, vision and bite. Peter Reid played the caricature of the foaming Scouse pit bull extremely well in central midfield but his ability to break up play and his short-range passing were sans pareil. Reid's midfield partner, Paul Bracewell, lent some elegance and vision. Then we had Kevin Sheedy. We could devote a whole book to Kevin Sheedy's left foot. Suffice to say it was 'elegant' and 'could open a tin of peas'. Then on the other flank there was the criminally underrated Trevor Steven; not only could he 'cover every blade of grass' but he had quality to burn. Has there been a better balanced English club side? We had two hopes. Bob Hope. And no hope. And Bob Hope was not in London.

TV cup final build-up on the big day went a bit like this:

9am: Flick through the *Radio Times* and decide whether you pick ITV or BBC for the coverage. Having seen that Jimmy Greaves (who was dead funny back then) was on ITV you quickly made your selection. You could always injudiciously switch back and forth during the commercial break and hope you caught the snooker final between Peter Reid and Bryan Robson.

9.01am–11am: Annoy the arse out of your mum waiting for the coverage to start. Annoy the arse out of your dad asking him who he thinks will win today 733 times. Be prepared to be sent to your room to play dice cricket around 9.05.

11am: Laugh heartily at Greavsie's comedy-sized rosette and Elton John glasses. Crack a rib or four each time he says 'It's a funny old game, Saint'.

11.20am: Join the teams at their respective hotels for breakfast. Watch Peter Reid eat a whole toaster. See the United lads each devour a 72oz steak, a shovel of chips, 17 fried eggs, a Desperate Dan shirt and two gallons of cream soda. 'We'll need plenty of energy today, Brian,' chirps Big Ron between mouthfuls.

11.45am: Cup final *Mastermind* with Peter Reid and Graeme Hogg.

11.46am: Join Elton Welsby on the Everton coach. Watch Elton embarrass Peter Reid with a picture of him waiting for Santa in a Liverpool kit aged five. Note how many players agree 'it will be a tough game today Elton'. Watch the chaos ensue as the local regional reporter no one has heard of tells us that 'United have had to go back to the team hotel as one or two players have the shits after breakfast'.

12pm: Watch Jimmy Tarbuck and Stan Boardman being interviewed as Big Ron and Howard Kendall respectively. Agree that Stan Boardman is funny, and that Jimmy Tarbuck is not. Wonder where Kenny Lynch is because he was funny last year.

12.10pm: Watch Anneka Rice fly over Wembley in a helicopter for no discernible reason.

12.25pm: Watch extended highlights of United's cup final training week with Greavsie in a tracksuit – laugh again. When the laughter has subsided note that Jimmy is the fittest of the United lads apart from Robbo. See how Big Ron offers 46-year-old Greavsie a contract: 'He still knows where the goal is, Elton. And he might bring a bit of much-needed pace up top.'

12.45pm: Meet the players with the respective captains. Give yourself a point for each time a player is referred to by a nickname. Find out who the joker in the pack is and which one wants to divorce his wife and live with Bo Derek.

1pm: The one we have been waiting for. The goal of the season competition result is announced. You entered by postcard a week ago. Find out you have not won. Agree that Jimmy Hill knows nothing about football and turn back to ITV.

1.10pm: Interview with Billy Connolly. He talks only about religion and shipbuilding in Govan, Glasgow. You wonder if he has the wrong ground as Celtic are playing up the road. 'Who is he, Dad? A comedian?' 'No son, he's not.'

1.20pm: It's time for the cup final songs. Chas and Dave funk up 'Glory, Glory, Man United'. Watch the Everton boys tracksuit and dad dance their way through 'Here We Go' with the multi-talented Kenny Lynch playing head tennis, riding a tricycle and performing backing vocals all at once.

1.30pm: Flick back to BBC for the *A Question of Sport* cup final special featuring Robbo and Whiteside on Bill's side and Peter Reid and Andy Gray on Emlyn's.

1.58pm: Watch Emlyn ask for 'number 6 please, Dave' in the second round of the picture board when it had already been opened and answered in the first round. Agree that Emlyn Hughes is a prized bellend. Turn back to ITV.

2.05pm: Watch the pundits (now augmented by Bobby Charlton and/or Bobby Robson and/or Mick Channon and/or Lawrie McMenemy) heartily agree that 'the FA Cup is the biggest competition in the world' and that 'it's a big day out for the fans'. Prepare to be reminded at least 13 times that 'Wembley is no place for losers'. Give yourself another point for each time someone says that 'Wembley is a big pitch and it can tie knots in muscles later on'.

2.20pm: Tactical analysis. 'United need to get long balls in to test the Everton defence,' says Big Jack.

2.21pm: Peek back to the BBC and watch Peter Reid edge out Robbo in the best-of-three snooker. A bad sign. Even in dicky bows.

2.45pm: 'Abide With Me'. Get your lyrics above.

Well? It was of its time and we loved it more than Sherbet Fountains and Rainbow Drops. Besides, even *Only Fools and Horses* has dated a bit. Feel sorry for my ten-year-old who has to contend with Robbie Savage, Jason

McAteer, Owen Hargreaves, Ian Wright, Alan Shearer, Michael Owen and Steve McManaman. I say that but he has his Nintendo Switch so doesn't have to bother before kick-off which these days is about midnight anyway. Maybe he is luckier than I thought. If he had been born ten years earlier, he'd have had to endure Dion Dublin and Peter Schmeichel. There is no joystick or games console invented that could save a kid of the noughties from Schmeichel's grey suit. Was that the only item of clothing in his wardrobe for about ten years? I had heard the BBC were poor payers in relation to their commercial competitors but this was taking the piss. I bet he had slip-on shoes as well.

On the morning of the final I, somewhat bewilderingly, eschewed all these fun and frolics in search of the greater good: a cup final programme. I think it had something to do with how I landed on the wrong end of a barter a couple of years earlier and somehow exchanged my Milk Cup Final programme for a dead goldfish and half a packet of Rainbow Drops. Quite how I expected to find an FA Cup Final programme in Warrington before kick-off time at Wembley is difficult to explain; while I couldn't find the tartan paint, I certainly had a long wait. Newsagent after newsagent said 'no'. They must have thought I was crazy, but they sensed my plaintive eyes and dutifully rummaged at the back amongst the chewing nuts and dirty mags. Programmes back then were currency. If you had a programme it was prima facie proof that you attended the game and as long as you knew a thing or two you could get away with it; up the social order you would go with every fresh *United Review* you could brandish at wet break. Years later a programme would get you a token and a number of tokens could get you a Wembley ticket. Brucie was right: points make prizes.

I arrived back cold and pissed off about 2pm. I was also getting the bug of the true supporter: nervous superstition. I had not watched any of the build-up, so I was not going to join in when it was three-parts done. This was serious business now; if Greavsie could not make me laugh what chance did Michael Barrymore have? I smashed a few snooker balls about in the garage. I threw a few arrows into the dartboard with the aggressive distractedness of Jocky Wilson himself. I flicked at the Subbuteo board, but I couldn't concentrate. Losing the FA Cup Final? When you're nine? It's unthinkable. Fast forward ten years to the day and it was United and Everton in the final again. We lost but I was too pissed and high to give a shit! Same the week before when we lost the league at West Ham. Besides, I was out with Hannah Davies that night which was far more important.

Here is the United side that played against Everton in the 1985 FA Cup Final at Wembley:

1. Gary Bailey
2. John Gidman
3. Arthur Albiston
4. Norman Whiteside
5. Paul McGrath
6. Kevin Moran
7. Bryan Robson (captain)
8. Gordon Strachan
9. Mark Hughes

10. Frank Stapleton
11. Jesper Olsen

Substitute:
12. Mike Duxbury.

I remembered a tight, uneventful game. As I mentioned earlier, Everton had played in Rotterdam just three days before. I think the Wembley pitch started to tie knots in their muscles as the game reached its denouement. It was a big pitch. The major turning point at 0-0 about 15 minutes from time was Kevin Moran's red card. It was curiously accepted back then that you had to double fracture or disembowel something to get a booking and bury bodies on Rillington Place to get a red. And it was against this torture chamber touchstone that all kinds of opprobrium were poured over referee Peter Willis for giving the notoriously rugged Irishman an early bath for a scything challenge on Peter Reid. It only clotheslined the Everton midfielder but denied a clear goalscoring opportunity. I have seen it a million times and, in any era, it is a red. Not even a Paul Merson orange.

What was even more striking was the reaction of the pundits to the dismissal, as neatly summarised in a Guardian.com article by Steven Pye published on 13 May 2013 and entitled 'Remembering the 1985 FA Cup Final – Manchester United v Everton'. Ian St John: 'I really do find that incredible Brian. I think the referee is 100 per cent out of order.'

Mick Channon was always prone to outbreaks of nonsense, but he excelled himself this day – maybe the pollen in the cup final flower had swollen his senses as well as his sinuses or he had some form of advanced equine flu? 'The game was nearly ruined by an impostor calling himself a referee.'

Even the nation's favourite comedian this side of Nelson Mandela House joined in the head stamping. Jimmy Greaves: 'He [the referee] wanted to get his name in history before he retired.' And criticism from such luminaries clearly turned poor Peter Willis towards some form of self-loathing schizophrenia: 'I have no second thoughts about sending off Kevin Moran. I believe I was right at the time and I still believe I was right. But that doesn't stop me feeling terrible about it.'

Why should he feel terrible? He was right. The 43 quid he got for the game makes this bollocks all the more risible. I wish more referees of today had his balls. Maybe they'd get more bloody respect? And players would learn to behave a bit better? It's probably a bit too late for all of that now.

In extra time I turned to the BBC for salvation. And then (probably for the first time but definitely not the last) I heard John Motson mutter the immortal line: 'It's sometimes harder to play against ten men than 11, Trevor.' What is he on about? He has just spent the last 100 minutes telling everyone how Wembley is such a big pitch and will tie knots in muscles later on. So how will losing a man help that? Please explain, John. He never did and he then spent years after trying to persuade us that a 2-0 lead is always problematical. I turned back to the wisdom of Brian Moore and Ian St John on the other side. Just in time to see Norman Whiteside's sweet curling shot evade the dive of Neville Southall.

I can't remember how long was left after Whiteside's goal – but I do recall disappearing to the landing upstairs: head in hands, hands in lap, unable to watch but knowing full well that the open door and Dad's gasps and groans would give it all away. It's a horrendous feeling that you may know yourself. Yet it's so hard to describe. Gut-wrenching? Stomach-churning? Yes, a bit, but it's more than that. It's like your black heart is about to explode into the stratosphere and only the sweat in your eyeballs is preventing a major cardiac crisis. The physical and emotional extremities of total investment. I could never watch David Gower bat: I was so bloody scared he would get out. Or Federer against Nadal. Or White against Hendry. Or O'Sullivan against anyone else. This is a sign of the quality people we really are: it is what separates us from the bores and braggarts; the PowerPointers and golfers; the neighbour watchers and talent recruitment coaches.

I knew of people at law school who sat chain-smoking in the common room all day when the results were on the noticeboard in the anteroom but that is not the same. That is a natural extension of circumstance, not a definition of who we are. But why did I care? It was in the bag all along wasn't it? 1-0 is safe; only if we made it two did we have a problem.

We hung on, just, and Robson lifted the cup again for United.

It was all about Kevin Moran in the end. First, we have John Gidman's romantic memories of sadly unrequited love in the 'Set Pieces' article by Andy Mitten published in *The Mirror* on 10 February 2015:

We were the underdogs. Everton were going for the treble and Big Ron told us, 'Don't sit back. Go at them.'

It was hot and we took salt tablets. The Wembley grass was long and I used longer studs than usual. When Peter Reid hit a volley, I stretched as far as I could to reach it, convinced the ball was going in. Somehow, my stud clipped it and it went wide.

It was a shocking decision to send Kevin off and I felt for him, but we still felt confident with ten men. With Frank Stapleton back at centre-half, we aimed for the replay until Norm the Storm did his bit and bent a winner around Neville Southall.

I was the first player to congratulate him and said: 'If there wasn't 100,000 people here I'd fuck you now.' After the game, I remember picking my old Villa team-mate Andy Gray up, a tear in his eye, and telling him to keep his head up.

I bet Moran was delighted – well worth missing a winners' medal, a royal well done and the 39 steps for. I wonder if Gidman shared his thoughts with HRH The Duke of Kent.

Act 6

It's What You Value

Wembley is no place for losers. There is a wonderful post-match ITV interview with Big Ron, Mark Hughes, Paul McGrath, Frank Stapleton and Norman Whiteside (again). Big Norm was asked by Jim Rosenthal to talk us through the goal: 'Mark done great. I just brought it inside on to my left foot, I just seen the gap and I just curled it.'

Brilliant! Milk as a celebration drink in 1983 and now this gold nugget! He could make the Grand Canyon sound like a second-hand Cortina. It was a brilliant goal but again the sending off took centre stage. Big Ron obviously was watching a different game: maybe he was wistfully dreaming of the one Venables was playing in Barcelona? Or maybe he simply didn't see it? Perhaps Arsène Wenger was assiduously making notes at home in France? 'The way I saw it I didn't even think that Kevin made an effort not to play for the ball.'

Personally, I didn't care a bit about the sending off. I sensed relief rather than joy. Relief and exhaustion. And when things settled down, a touch of that warm glow of satisfaction which beats joy any day of the week. It sounds perverse but United victories always felt a deeply personal achievement for me. It was as if I had been kicking the balls out there. I always felt a bit disconnected from the exams I passed as if someone else was writing the answers. But is that so bizarre? I was kicking every ball for United. And the teachers desperate for me to succeed provided me with the answers which I memorised and trotted out. There is more of me in those United wins than in any GCSE or A level pass.

Indeed, not everyone was so euphoric. In the interview mentioned above Paul McGrath, though featured, did not say a single word. Nor did Mark Hughes. He explained his post-match emotions to Brian Viner of *The Independent* in an article published on 19 January 2007: 'I've watched the video back, and I can see myself sort of half jumping up and down, thinking "I wish this was over". All I could think was "let them get this song out of the way, then I can scurry back to the dressing-room".'

Ron Atkinson once described him as better than Tony Adams and John Terry put together and I wouldn't disagree. But he was black in a country where the only other black stuff was swilled in industrial quantities and regularly spat out with the venom and prejudices of the times. No wonder he struggled on the life side of the white line.

The season ended with events which put the pursuit of silverware firmly into context: the Bradford stadium fire, and the Heysel disaster. I'd like to say I'd have traded the FA Cup to avert both but back then I'd probably be lying. Through the blinkered eyes of a nine-year-old football fundamentalist I couldn't comprehend how one club's actions cost my club the chance of glory on the European stage. And I still can't. Why not just ban Liverpool? Why ban Everton? Why ban us? Why ban Spurs? Why ban Southampton? What had we all done wrong? Were we at Heysel that night? It arguably ruined Everton as a club. Denied a shot at the European Cup which they could have won. For the record, the very average Steaua Bucharest won it in 1986 ... They could have built a dynasty with that side. One minute they are in the European Cup and the next minute they are not. One minute they have Howard Kendall and Gary Lineker, the next they have Colin Harvey and Mike Newell. And it's not their fault. None of it. It's no wonder the blue noses are as bitter as a bad pint.

As we have said it's always good to build on an FA Cup success. Truth be told, when we bought no one that piss-wet summer of 1985 I hardly noticed. The second love of my life had been born: cricket. It was 1985 and the Ashes: the swashbuckling Ian Botham and criminally talented David Gower facing Allan Border's men in one of the longest-running rivalries in sport. When I was told it was over a burnt piece of wood I was hooked. They say no one likes desperation, and maybe that's true, but some good things are borne out of it; sometimes I think it is difficult to find the confidence to be yourself when you still feel you have an element of choice. Look at Nirvana: Kurt was Kurt because he had to be, not because it was what he wanted. We all want to be accepted but some of us never will be. When we know that, it's easier to find our true voice because we then know that's all we have.

Kurt would have been a great United fan, I think. And it's not just about weirdos like you and me. How many great business ideas are a last throw of the dice when you've failed at everything else? When you have long since ceased giving a shit.

Anyway, I was so bored without football in the summer that I idly tuned in to Richie, Tony Lewis and the boys. There was no choice but to give it a go. In a world before constant push-button entertainment when the only buttons ever pushed were those of our constantly pissed-off mothers, we had to make our own fun. Do you remember the vernacular? 'Go out and play and don't come back till 5.' 'Entertain yourselves.' 'Children should be seen and not heard.' And if you breathed a toast topper of dissent: 'Wait till your father gets home!' These days it's the kids in control. They critically inspect the itinerary in advance making red-line strikethroughs in their agile minds: 'Dad, do we have to do finger painting, ice skating, rollerblading, crazy golf, white-water rafting, indoor skiing, rope swinging, dinosaur hunting and go to the zoo and Pizza Express today? Can I not just have £250 for Roblox instead?' Why my parents ever complained about being tired defeats me. They don't know the meaning of the bloody word. Try writing this after a day doing law and a weekend doing finger painting, ice skating, rollerblading, crazy golf, white-water rafting, indoor skiing, rope swinging, dinosaur hunting and going to the zoo and Pizza Express. 'Wait till your father gets home' now only tells a third of the story. The second part is: 'He's got a Switch game each for you.' Then their response: 'Has he bought any Lego from Argos?'

As the August wickets flattened and Gower's form picked up, the Charity Shield hardly got a look-in. A strong Everton side now containing Gary Lineker beat us 2-0. The portents were hardly good that day: Graeme Hogg and Mike Duxbury in the same side.

While Big Ron may be forgiven for not strengthening a couple of years earlier, not doing so now was not so easy to overlook. Why not sign Terry Fenwick from QPR or Terry Butcher from Ipswich? Both England international defenders who surely would have jumped at the prospect of signing for United from more unfashionable environs. Why not break the bank for Gary Lineker? Lineker was proven at First Division level now – a guaranteed bag of goals that we badly needed. Granted Everton were champions but there was no European Cup, so it probably was up for grabs. United was the bigger name. So, charm him. Show him round the ground. Wine and dine him. Pay for him and his wife to go to Barbados or Mexico (where no doubt Big Ron was doing media work for ITV rather than getting the deal done for United). Show him the European Cup from 1968. Get Bobby Charlton to have lunch with him. In fact, forget that. Give him a ten-year contract. Make him the best-paid player in Britain apart from Robson. Buy him an XR3i. A lifetime supply of Sharp electronics equipment of his choice. Free fish and chips at Lou Macari's on non-matchdays. Get Robson in his ear. But do something. Anything. A 42-hurdle steeplechase requires a thoroughbred striker. Not Alan 'Bloody' Brazil.

All of which made Big Ron's preseason rhetoric seem like, well, exactly that: rhetoric. He said the below at the

time, as recalled by John Spurling in a *FourFourTwo* article
published on 13 January 2017.

> There's little doubt that football stands at a
> crossroads, and it's now even more important
> to remember that football should be all about
> entertainment. At Old Trafford, we're aiming to
> put the smile back on people's faces.
>
> I'm obsessed about finishing ahead of Liverpool
> and Everton. If we do that, we'll be the 1986 league
> champions – no question.

He spoke well. He was media-savvy at a time when
publicists only worked for Joan Collins and Blake
Carrington. He appreciated perhaps more than the rest
of us that the post-Heysel football terrain would be harsh
and uncompromising: it was serious business with talk of
banning away fans and imposing booze bans at grounds.
The rest? Pure bollocks? How can you be obsessed about
challenging Liverpool and Everton with Graeme Hogg,
Mike Duxbury and Alan Brazil in the side? It makes no
sense, especially after a sun-drenched summer of complete
inertia.

After the Charity Shield pasting it was Aston Villa at
Old Trafford on the opening day. We were holidaying in
Cornwall at the time and as Dad was colourfully seasick
on an unfeasibly unsafe mackerel boat, I couldn't help
thinking how we were getting on. I needn't have worried
– a 4-0 smattering of the Villains with a Mark Hughes
double. Big Ron was never one to get carried away, was he?
One swallow and all that? As recalled in John Spurling's

FourFourTwo article Big Ron had his feet firmly in the Liverpool and Everton sky: 'We looked fluid and menacing throughout,' he purred. 'To be so rhythmic early in the season is very pleasing.'

He must have forgotten how turgid we were at Wembley seven days before; I'm sure he blamed the Band Aid lot for messing up the pitch you know. Feed the world? No way! Charity begins at home, Bob. But there was no *Match of the Day* to see us smash up Villa. 'Why's that, Dad?' I asked as his arsehole hit the bottom of the English Channel. He never replied. The story of why not is actually quite interesting. The Football League had rejected an offer of £19m over four years to show 19 live matches a season. The clubs insisted no more than 13 live games and so the impasse followed. It seems a million years ago. Sky and BT now show 19 live games in a weekend, albeit for a few more quid. The dick swinging betrayed an uncertainty as to where the balance of power lay. Did football need TV? Or did TV need football? We now know that it's a symbiotic thing but back then, according to the Tory gutter press, football was a dirty game watched by dirty hooligans in dirty pens. The national broadcasters were determined to use political rhetoric to force the price down.

In comments reproduced in a *Guardian* sports article by Steven Pye dated 3 December 2019 the BBC's then head of sport, Jonathan Martin, and his counterpart at ITV, John Bromley, made their feelings clear: 'Football rates itself far too highly,' said Martin. 'It has no God-given right to be on television.' 'We are prepared to renegotiate,' said ITV head of sport John Bromley. 'But it's up to them to approach us and we shall only be able

to offer them substantially less than our original offer.'
'Recorded football is a dead duck,' he continued. 'The days
when *The Big Match* or *Match of the Day* kept people in on
a Sunday afternoon or Saturday night are over. The public
don't want it anymore. They want live action.'

He was right. We did want live action, but I suspect
he had no idea that someone outside of the establishment
would be prepared to pay a fair price for it. You never
know when the new young buck will appear from round
the corner, rip up your cosy monopoly and expose your
lazy stereotypes.

After Aston Villa, two away wins followed at Ipswich
(including Terry Butcher) and Arsenal. So, there we were:
top of the table after three matches with maximum points.
Mark Hughes had scored three in three and Lineker was
not yet off the mark for Everton. Our fourth game was at
home to West Ham on the occasion of my tenth birthday:
Bank Holiday Monday, 26 August 1985. I desperately
wanted to go, and my dad knew it. He had taken me to
City when I was about six; I remember watching them
destroy Leeds and narrowly defeat Notts County in the
1981/82 season and then draw against Spurs the following
year. In early 1985 he took me to Anfield to see Liverpool
annihilate Norwich, only because his club game was called
off and Liverpool, unlike Rylands FC of Warrington, had
undersoil heating. I'm not sure Dad had ever been to Old
Trafford himself at that point. Why would he unless he
was in City colours? And while he was brave, he was not a
fool. It was a bit tasty in the 70s by all accounts. I had also
been to Wembley in March 1984, but it was shit. One of
those England Schoolboy games you go to with your club

side: all Smiths crisps and air horn klaxons that stupid girls who had too much sugar on the coach sounded every two seconds to piss you off. The only thing I do remember was Damian Garrington launching an apple he had only just bitten into about 50 rows down and it crowning some unsuspecting poor sod in the process. St John Ambulance, blood, concussion, the lot. He laughed about it on the way home with his half-ham, half-cheese milk roll sandwiches, YoYo biscuit and Panda Pop.

Birthdays when you are young are odd things. You unwisely disregard the evidence of the bitter past. So while I wanted United tickets and a home strip, I always got a pencil case, a protractor, a compass, a shatterproof ruler, an italic pen and a bottle of Quink ink; people obviously had one eye on the imminent return to school but it was my fucking birthday you know! Why not just go the whole hog and wrap up the school uniform? Or the PE kit? The CDT apron? The Home Economics basket? Would you have done the same if my birthday was on 7 November or 5 February? The one thing I wouldn't have minded was the Dunlop Amber or Green Flash trainers, but I never got them. There was always hope. Maybe this would be the year. But maybe Warrington Town would win the FA Vase? I went upstairs to sulk, in silence; Oscar-winning performances were simply not tolerated back then. I did not want to risk the chicken curry and egg-fried rice which would probably arrive later on. During my internal fulminations I neglected to notice an envelope being placed under my door 'from RA'. 'Who the fuck was RA?' I thought. It was four tickets to the match. I couldn't have been more elated; well, actually, I could have been. A lot more. Why the hell was my sister going? She didn't deserve a fucking ticket; she'd just piss me off on the way there with her Duran Duran tape. A home strip to grace the occasion would not have gone astray either, especially as the four tickets only cost 12 quid – adults four quid, kids two quid. It was the parents back then who didn't know they were born.

The tickets were for the L stand, or the family stand as it was more affectionately known; it was sponsored by Panini stickers but this was my birthday not the harvest festival so I got none of those; you'd have thought that RA (whoever he was) might have slipped a couple of packets into the envelope but that didn't materialise. Thatcher thought we were all filthy animals, of course, but that barn dance, 'What's the story northern Tory' family stand probably contained more Conservatives than the Boat Race. Of course, she wouldn't have known that most First Division grounds had a family stand; nor would she have cared.

She decided the outcome in advance without reference to the facts or the evidence and then installs some sycophantic, shiny-arsed minister in a grey suit to do the dirty work. Not that the West Ham fans were too bothered about the FTSE price or the Single European Act babble. They hurled missile after missile at anything in red. Fortunately those in the K stand were directly above the Hammers and were happy to empty piping-hot coffee, tea, beer, spit and God knows what else on them. Why would you pick a fight with a bloke towering above you when he has a thermos flask and you can't grow the requisite 10m in height? Insanity.

I recall on ascending the steps to the family stand that my dad made me pause, theatrically, before I entered the stadium for the first time. His words: 'You will never forget this.' And he was right. The year before against Watford I couldn't see a bloody thing (and I'm pretty sure someone pissed in my pocket as well) but this time I had the full panorama: the sheer scale and size of the place, the pitch in shades of the most verdant green I had ever seen, the songs, the atmosphere (there were 50,773 crammed into Old Trafford that day), the symbiosis between the players and fans during the warm-up, the whiff of hot dog and fried onions (I never got to taste one – it was my birthday not the harvest festival). I took it all in and clutched my *United Review* programme as if it was Brink's-Mat gold. If life is measured by just a number of moments this was one.

We had to win that day. Mind you, if we didn't I wouldn't have cared that much; once someone has let you into their soul or stadium you love them more after they have fucked up and showed you their vulnerable side. A 2-0 regulation win courtesy of goals from Strachan and Hughes meant four wins from four. We were now clear at the top. Even my dad conceded (Olsen and Bailey excepted) we were a 'good side' – he failed to eulogise about the Brazilian sides of 1970 and 1982 so he must have had a point – dads always do when you're ten; shame about the rest. I can't remember a thing about any of the United players that day. Frank McAvennie caught my eye far more than Olsen or Strachan or Robson: a blond bombshell – all energy, pace and movement. Maybe it was just the blond hair? My dad always said that strong features made a player stand out. Scouts, he said, are always likely to remember a player with ginger hair or coloured boots or the gobshite one who shouts and pretends to organise at the back. Mark Ward was really good as well. Around this time, I semi-rhetorically asked Stoney (remember him, my Liverpool mate?) who his favourite player was: 'Mark Ward – West Ham,' he replied unequivocally. I thought he might be after my Dairylea Triangle or 54321 biscuit, but he was probably being sincere. Ward was a fine player who never hit the heights.

We went on to the City Ground on 31 August where Cloughie's lot were vanquished 3-1. Whereas hyperbole was common currency from Big Ron you wouldn't think the normally level-headed Frank Stapleton would depart from the usual platitudes. But it was contagious. As recalled in Jon Spurling's *FourFourTwo* article, the Irishman was euphoric after the Forest victory:

> This is a very, very exciting situation which we find ourselves in.

> We've won our first five fixtures, and although no one is getting carried away, we believe we can carry on with this run. I moved here from Arsenal to be a winner. The others feel the same. This is our chance.

Five wins only Frank; 37 matches to go. Had they never heard of the swings and roundabouts of marathons and sprints in Dublin's fair city? Good to see the boys were not getting carried away though … Newcastle were then defeated at home 3-0: Stapleton (2) and Hughes.

Mark Hughes had now scored six in six and topped the goalscoring charts. I knew we were right not to sign Gary Lineker. We only conceded two goals in those first six games. I knew we were right not to sign Terry Butcher and Terry Fenwick. We then beat Oxford United at home, Man City away and West Brom at home. It was nine from nine. A narrow home victory over Southampton courtesy of another Mark Hughes goal in late September made it ten from ten. Can you believe it? I couldn't but just like an after-hours piss-up with your boss I always sensed nothing good would come from it. Perhaps Ron Atkinson too had hit Ron Bacardi with Martin Edwards and told a few unwise tales which he regretted the next day. Certainly, he was uncharacteristically reticent after win number ten (Jon Spurling, *FourFourTwo*, again): 'It's magnificent, but the league is a marathon, not a sprint. We know we can't continue winning forever, and the key will be to pick ourselves up after we stumble.'

I'd like to say we looked irresistible but there was still no breakthrough in the broadcasting war, ergo no *Match of the Day*. Ain't it fair, eh? United's best-ever start, and no one saw hide nor hair of it. Round about this time, Frank McAvennie, who had scored a bucketful of goals for West Ham that season, was taken on Waterloo Bridge by Martin Tyler and no one recognised him apart from a cabbie (who know everyone and everything anyway so do not count). Billy Connolly spied him on the South Bank as well, but he knows everyone and everything as well – he'd have been a great cabbie if he wasn't busy talking about religion and shipbuilding in Govan, Glasgow. It makes you realise the significance of *Match of the Day*, and how important TV was to the broader fabric of the game, even back then. As for United? Well, there's a legal principle I have often misapplied over the years: *res ipsa loquitur*, meaning 'the thing speaks for itself'. The results do not lie. It was obvious that McGrath was the best defender in the world, that Robson was avoiding accidents and playing out of his skin, that Hughes was scoring for fun. We didn't need to see it. We knew that the skies were blue, that the grass was green, that the Panda Pops were warm and that attendances were up, with all but one of the first five home league games attracting gates of more than 50,000. We didn't need anyone to tell us it was sunshine and lollipops at Old Trafford.

If you can ignore the sky-blue baby pictures and flapjack fingerprints, my school project from October 1985 said it all. Things that make me happy: 'when United win and Liverpool and Everton lose'. Things that make me sad: 'when United lose and Liverpool and Everton win'. It was safe to assume I'd put the cricket pads away. We headed to Kenilworth Road to take on Luton Town in early October 1985. One more win would equal Bill Nicholson's record start to the season over 20 years before, a season which saw Spurs collect an unprecedented league and cup double. It had a cup final feel to it – almost like we had to win even when we didn't if that makes sense? History and momentum are powerful things when they suddenly slam on the anchors or start to work against you. Grappenhall Sports Under 11s had training that afternoon, after which we were allowed up to the first-team bar with a blackcurrant and water each to watch the scores roll in: 1-1. It felt like a damaging loss. I was very quick to ascribe blame. The plastic pitch for one. How can you play football on plastic in trainers? Was that what God intended? Burnt legs and twisted ankles? I was definitely right to raise that point. Steve Foster was a more dubious argument. I blamed the Luton captain's headband. Who plays football in a headband? It's not fucking Wimbledon mate! He also, I think, started that not shaving bollocks during a cup run. So, he ends up looking like ZZ Top at Wembley and failing to see the ball. Bloody idiot. Maybe I overreacted a touch. We won three out of the next four and were miles ahead at the top when the implacable November weather arrived: played 15; won 13; drawn two.

We lost our undefeated record and Bryan Robson to injury in the piss and mud of Hillsborough on 9 November 1985. A ten-point lead cut to seven and shorn of our best player. Robson would not appear again until February 1986, by which time we had tailed off and Liverpool and Everton were moving ominously into form. And to make matters a good deal worse we lost at Anfield in the Milk Cup in late November. Paul McGrath (now excelling in midfield) put us ahead but a Jan Mølby double was enough for Liverpool – a fine player he was. Just as I began to practise a cough and 'that sick voice' Dad threw a white rag at me. I don't know whether he found it somewhere and there were no socks or shorts, but I didn't care for that; nor did I care it was the away shirt. It was my first United shirt and I loved it. Check it out – United away 1984–86. I wore it to school the next day. My Broomfields Junior School shirt was white too and the red Sharp writing must have resembled a beacon. Mr Greenwood was not colour-blind, but he was a United fan and maybe he understood; perhaps he was hurting too. That shirt-wearing defiance was an emotional turning point. Next day after a defeat you do not cry and cower; you turn up strong and proud. It's odd how we had great strips when we were shit but when we turned great the kits turned shit. Do you remember that yellow and green away shirt from 1993/94? Be honest, who really cared about Newton Heath anyway? The grey monstrosity from 1995/96? And its illegitimate bastard son of a blue third strip? The relationship between poor presentation and excellent results is a mystery. I'm sensing you don't believe me. OK, well explain this. How come you are falling over and wading through women when you are a drunk, dissolute, shambling wreck but when you tidy up and sort your act out, they disappear. Go on then? Women and Man United! Who'd have them?

The year 1986 dawned with A-ha, Shakin' Stevens and Dirty Den rampant and kids all over the land glued to *Chuckie Egg 2* and *Grange Hill*. But for United fans it arrived pregnant with the expectation that the 19-year title hoodoo would be broken. Maybe it was the lemonade shandies or the brandy snaps talking but, despite an indifferent run, on Wednesday, 1 January 1986 we were still five points clear at the top, with a game in hand; we had not left top spot all season. Regulation victories followed against Birmingham City and Oxford United. Not even a home defeat against Nottingham Forest in mid-January knocked us off the perch.

Robson returned on 2 February 1986 for our live televised Sunday away game against West Ham (the broadcasters and the Football League had now reached some kind of uneasy truce). He scored a wonderful goal to put us ahead, then injured his shoulder again and went off. We lost 2-1. We were now second. Robson was done. The damage was done. And what amidst such machinations does Big Ron do? He agrees to sell Mark Hughes (leading scorer) to Barcelona.

In John Spurling's *FourFourTwo* article Hughes admitted that the deal sanctioned by Atkinson in January but kept secret from journalists and fans until the end of the season 'destroyed my concentration'.

Hughes expanded on this in a 'One-on-One' *FourFourTwo* article published in May 2007:

> I was on something like £250 a week and still living in digs. I couldn't afford to move out even though I'd been playing in the first team for 18 months. In the September before I left, a new contract put me up to £1,000 a week, but the situation just snowballed. I met the Barcelona people around January of the year I left [1986]; I was talking to one of the greatest clubs in the world and I was thinking 'I really don't want to be here.' But I was led a certain way and before I knew it, I signed. Even up to getting on the plane to move out there, I was thinking maybe something will change and I won't actually go. As it was, I ended up on the plane, but it wasn't for the money.

So, we have a 22-year-old striker who loves the bones of the club he has grown up at; he is adored by the fans; he is scoring goals for fun; he is happy. He is pressured to leave, and it fucks up his form for the remainder of the season, a season which, with him focused, may well have been a championship-winning season. Look at the evidence: Hughes bagged ten in the first 15 games but only another seven that whole season. Big Ron referred to it as 'a temporary problem for a young player'. He knew better. He knew the reason why. He knew Hughes's mind was elsewhere. Of course, it would be. A 22-year-old lad being jettisoned from a home he loves to God knows where against his will. How would you react? And fine, I accept fully he was paid to make big decisions but as I tell young lawyers, what's the next step? It's no good losing the £5m Barclays contract and then telling me that John Pickles might be interested in a small claim against his landlord as long as it can be done on a 'no win, no fee' agreement. No good at all.

In two separate acts of John Pickles's monumental idiocy, Big Ron bought Terry Gibson from Coventry City in January 1986 for £600,000, and Peter Davenport from Nottingham Forest in March 1986 for £750,000. Barcelona paid £1.8 million for Mark Hughes and he replaced him with those two, leaving us with enough change to buy a Dip Dab and a Mint Aero. OK, so Robson only played 21 out of 42 league games (and only six of the last 26) but we needed goals as well. Liverpool had Rush and Dalglish; Everton had Lineker and Sharpe; Chelsea had Dixon and Speedie; even West Ham had Cottee and McAvennie for Cliff's sake. We had a justifiably pissed-off Mark Hughes and Frank Stapleton who only scored seven all season. And as for Gibson and Davenport? Gibson scored an astonishing one goal in 23 for United; Davenport in comparison was rapier sharp (22 in 92). And you think that's hindsight?

Not one bit. Neither were prolific beforehand. Go on, do it! Everyone else does. Maybe they struggled in the Old Trafford goldfish bowl? That bloody goldfish bowl! Maybe it was all fairground plastic bags in Coventry and Nottingham? Oh, did I mention John Sivebaek, who we bought in the winter of 1985? Another Great Dane. Just what you needed to replace Robson: a central midfield player with the engine of Neil Webb and the vision of Mike Phelan. You have to be a proper United supporter or have a heart of stone to read the above without laughing.

Spring 1986 was a funny old time. Zammo McGuire was on heroin on *Grange Hill*. How could he do that to the lovely Jackie Wright? The 'Just Say No' song featuring Fay Lucas, Ziggy Greaves and Rowland Browning on backing vocals and Kev Baylon's rap hit the top ten and the bigger campaign had reached the rarefied air of Reagan's Oval Office. But, just like every other utterly perplexed ten-year-old, I couldn't fathom exactly what I was supposed to 'say no' to. Liverpool? England? Ron Atkinson? Gola trainers? I didn't need an inducement to say no to any of them. Besides, who was going to sell me heroin at ten years of age? Where was I going to get the money from? If I went within a ten-mile radius of Richard Moorfield's B&H Dad would know and he would kill me. Escalation is irrelevant when you are in the boneyard. And when we weren't dealing with this American-infused nonsense, we had *Spitting Image* and 'The Chicken Song' shoving deckchairs up your nose. Maybe that was the designer drug to avoid?

Then there was the Chernobyl Armageddon where we were told that acid rain would kill us before a ball was kicked in that summer's World Cup. I can remember hunchback dinner assistants with porcine features ringing bells to call a halt to the delicately poised playground derby. They only tried once; we would sooner die of sulphuric poisoning than lose to that lot with time still on the clock. In a season of vicissitudes a win at Old Trafford over Chelsea in April would have sent us back to the top (so, of course, we lost) and four days later we lost again at home, this time to the might of Howard Wilkinson's Sheffield Wednesday. And when Stoney came into school on Monday singing 'Just Another Manic Wednesday' it was time to search for last year's cricket stumps in the dank tea chest.

Kevin Moran explained to Jon Spurling in *FourFourTwo*: 'We lost our shape and our width.' That is overcomplicating things. We lost our best player and main goalscorer – it is that stark. To suggest that the key to the title lay with Jesper Olsen and Peter Barnes is fanciful: these were dilettantes who lacked the rain-soaked, mud-caked consistency that a 42-game season required back then. It was probably around this time that the lazy journalists promulgated rumours about the drinking brigade at United. You regularly heard that the Liverpool lads drank as hard. Big Ron explained this to Ian Herbert of *The Independent* in an article dated 15 September 2016: 'Under me Manchester United were a team that were supposed to have drunk themselves into oblivion, usually at the Four Seasons Hotel by [Manchester] airport.' 'That was a massive exaggeration. Alcohol was part of the temper of the times in English football and it was not confined to Manchester United. I once joined Liverpool on a post-season tour to Israel and I could not believe the amounts of booze that team put away; even those you wouldn't suspect were big drinkers, like [Alan] Hansen. Everton won two championships with Howard Kendall taking his team to Chinatown most Tuesday afternoons.'

There may be an element of self-justification in this, but the context and the detail provided suggest the veracity of the account. I also have it on good authority that one Liverpool player of the times convinced himself after marriage that drink was no longer an issue as 'I just have six or seven pints after a game now with the missus and a meal'. But alcohol is only part of discipline. Were we training as hard in between? It is difficult to envisage Dalglish or Kendall arriving at preseason training with a valise case containing a radio, smoked salmon and Ambre Solaire: it would have been a holiday gin or two, then down to hard work. I remember when John Barnes arrived at Liverpool he was told by Ronnie Moran (not Dalglish) that they trained in shorts whatever the weather: 'play in shorts, train in shorts'. Barnes followed suit. So, the Boot Room prevailed over the best player in the country. Something tells me the United boys would have been tracksuited up well before the trick or treaters knocked on the manager's door looking for Quality Street. A training ground contretemps between Remi Moses and Jesper Olsen left the former with bruised knuckles and the latter with 11 stitches under his left eye. Again. Could you imagine this happening on Merseyside in 1986?

Stan Boardman had it about right when he said, 'United managed to finish fourth in a two-horse race.' He was half-right, save that we had finished fourth in what should have been a one-horse canter. Gordon Strachan was spot on too in John Spurling's *FourFourTwo* article: 'Ron proved that he couldn't manage that team to the title,' he explained, 'and something had to change.'

Strangely, perhaps, I had little or no interest in England's efforts at the Mexico World Cup. I didn't even care about the handball goal: he's the greatest player ever and it is typical English hypocrisy of the worst brand that Lineker would have been knighted for what Maradona did. There is a lot of big-club syndrome about it. If you support Rotherham or Portsmouth or Walsall, you have a season-long break from pressure and anticipation. You know what will happen in May in August. We are exhausted by the end of the campaign; even if you can have a nap and recharge in La Manga for a week or two you still have a squad full of Liverpool players to cheer on. It doesn't feel right, and football is an emotional game. It must be more by accident than design that no one has been murdered on England duty: how can you forget someone's true allegiance which is branded all over their bone marrow like Blackpool rock? No England shirt can disguise that; nor should it. Maybe it's just me? Mind you, we all know full well that if the World Cup was in the Tesco Metro 50 yards down the road England would have a panic attack on the motor scooter. Where's the fun in that? Especially when you have Ian Botham's blond streaks and drug ban, David Gower's cover drive and Richard Hadlee's through-the-gate off-cutter to adore and admire. Not to mention Richie Benaud's cream suits and slip-ons. It was time to find the Gunn and Moore Skipper bat and the linseed oil.

Act 6a

I Remember Jeep

It was a weird old summer as well. I was 11 now; it was big school in September. Things were changing. I quite liked the look of Julie Black who was a friend of a friend and I spent some days with her at the park and library, sharing Hula Hoops and chips from the Neptune Bar when she managed to roll her dad for 35p. I also started to hang out with one or two lads who were into their tunes. One mate of mine called David Flynn had a mum with a new husband who was keen to impress and get us out of the way: he would send us upstairs with The Beatles and Bob Dylan vinyl and a few more things besides. It wasn't long before I was humming about 'Strawberry Fields' and having 'Visions of Johanna' and Dad was wondering where he had gone right. Still, football was still my first love and I was ready to go again by August.

When a chairman has to speak out in support of his manager before a ball has been kicked in anger you know there's trouble at Old Trafford. In comments reproduced in a *Guardian* article by Steven Pye dated 3 October 2018

Martin Edwards proffered the dreaded 'vote of confidence' before the start of the 1986/87 campaign: 'Obviously, it's been a long time without the league title and the longer it goes the more the pressure builds up on everyone at the club. But to keep harping on about it doesn't help the management or the players.'

Not exactly a ringing endorsement is it? There was some suggestion that Edwards was unhappy that Big Ron was in Mexico commentating in the World Cup summer of 1986 when he felt he should be in Manchester – fair point.

I can remember we lost at home to newly promoted Charlton (yes, at home to newly promoted Charlton) to secure our third loss in three. We were nothing if not consistent: we were 100 per cent at the same stage the season before, remember? I recall watching my dad's game that blustery afternoon. Steve Slater was the star player on the Greenalls team and a bit of a hero with his rakish moustache and pace and goals. I often wondered why he was not playing for United: if you can score a hat-trick away at Ditton, why not at home to Charlton? He was no Mark Hughes but surely a better option than Davenport, Brazil or Gibson? He was a huge United fan too. I used to warm up with him where he tried in vain to get me to use my left foot: 'You'll never be short of a game if you have a left foot, Jamie.' To curry favour with him I would endeavour to keep him up to date with all things United during the game: this would secure me smoky bacon crisps and a coke in a glass bottle in The Cross Keys after the game. Question: why does Coca-Cola always taste better in a glass bottle?

'How did we get on, Jamie?'

'1-0, Slate.'

'Jesus. 1-0 against that lot? Who scored?'

'Dunno.'

'How do you know we scored then?'

'We didn't. 1-0 Charlton. I don't know any of their players, Slate.'

'Charlton? We lost at home to Charlton? Fucking Charlton? Fucking joke.'

Edwards was not for turning, certainly not yet: 'We are not fickle enough to sack a manager on the strength of three games.'

Early autumn was not all crunchy leaves and thicker socks. In mid to late September 1986 I remember arriving back home after my perfect Geoff Hurst hat-trick against Penlake (header, right foot, left foot) to watch us take on Everton at Goodison Park live on the BBC. As we were driving back home Robson equalised for United. 'Hello! Hello! United are back! United are back! Hello!' I merrily sang as I opened the tricky garage door to sling my Nike Typhoon boots and Puma shin pads into the dark and dank for another few days. Everton went ahead before hands were washed and won 3-1. Jimmy Hill after the game implored Ron to 'have a good weekend'. Cheers, Jim. Not much left of it though at ten to five on a Sunday. Another defeat as well and the boardroom tomorrow morning. It will be great.

At least the journey home would spare him the desperate agony of *Last of the Summer Wine* which may have made a sacking unnecessary.

The next week we were live on TV again: at home to Chelsea on ITV. My hat-trick this day was against Rope and Anchor – lots of hat-tricks but never a match ball … We lost 1-0 and missed two penalties in the space of two minutes: first Olsen, then Strachan. I can recall the ITV reporter boneheadedly asking the Chelsea keeper, Tony Godden, after the game whether he had any sympathy for United. 'None. They should have signed me on a free in the summer.' Fair point: we had Chris Turner in goal that day. 'This is the worst position I have been in as a football manager,' said Atkinson as he reflected on the 1-0 defeat. 'We have got to buckle down and start winning matches.'

Big Ron was ready to go by early November. The sword of Damocles finally fell after a loss to Southampton away in the League Cup. In the 'Set Pieces' article by Andy Mitten published on 10 February 2015 Big Ron proudly boasted: 'I had five years in charge at United, spent a few quid and did enough shrewd business to get most of it back.' Sixteen words and then we move on, I promise. Terry Gibson and Peter Davenport and Mark Hughes and John Sivebaek and Alan Brazil and Arthur Graham and Peter Beardsley and David Platt. OK, that's 23 words of 'shrewd business'.

In an interview with Jonathan Shrager of StrettyNewsTV published on 8 November 2017 Martin Edwards set out a fair and well-balanced critique of Big Ron's tenure and the reasons behind his departure:

> I think Ron's period was a bit like Tommy Doherty's. It was exciting but you never quite felt we were quite a league-winning side. And I think

with Ron, two great cup runs there. Winning the FA Cup was still big in those days. It was bigger in those days than it is today actually, the FA Cup.

We were never out of the top four. We qualified for Europe every year he was there so Ron was certainly not a failure. But at the end I think when we finally made the decision, we were 19th in the table. We'd started the season badly and it was the worse time of his tenure at the end. After 4–5 good years I just felt we were going backwards rather than forwards. And I couldn't see us winning the league under Ron. So, decided to make the change.

Totally right.

And Fergie arrived and the rest is history? Or is it? If it was then you could all go off now and read that Proust novel you want to read but never will. I've often wondered who else they had in mind? It would have to be a British manager; it was still the milky tea with sugar days: no one would accept Arsène Wenger's pasta, water and vitamin revolution in 1986. The union rep would be on the phone to Gordon Taylor at the PFA and he'd have the chocolate Hobnobs out before you could say Bonjour Tristesse. Who said there was no player power back then. Howard Kendall? He was at Everton and frankly he would not have left Everton for United at that time. Who did that leave? Davie Hay at Celtic? Could Graeme Souness be tempted down from Ibrox? Terry Venables from Barcelona? How about England manager Bobby Robson who suffered some egregious treatment by the media? In a *Telegraph* article by John MacLeary published on 10 June 2009 Jim Leighton revealed that Fergie almost took the Arsenal job in the summer of 1986:

> Ferguson was offered the Arsenal job.
>
> George Graham would have been his assistant, but he wanted to wait until the World Cup was finished before it was getting announced.
>
> Arsenal said they wanted it [a decision] straight away and so he refused it and George Graham got the job.
>
> He wanted to announce it when he got back to Aberdeen, to do it the right way.

Gerry Armstrong adds to the plot: 'I knew he was lined up at Tottenham, maybe a year before that.'

Circumstance and timing are everything in football, as in life. Jock Stein tragically died from a heart attack after Scotland's World Cup qualifier with Wales back in September 1985, following which Ferguson agreed to combine the Scotland job with his Aberdeen duties until after the World Cup in Mexico: maybe Billy Connolly turned down the role? No doubt he would have succeeded where Ally MacLeod failed and brought the trophy back from South America, if he wasn't tied up talking about religion and shipbuilding in Govan, Glasgow. So, if Ferguson wasn't the proud Scotsman then he may have ended up in the Highbury hot seat. Imagine that you Arsenal fans? No George Graham? No Arsène Wenger? Your two greatest managers. But maybe an even greater one? Perhaps a Champions League or two? How does that make you feel? The Emirates might now be the Theatre of

Dreams and we might be languishing in mid-table looking to offload Mesut Özil. We may never have recovered from appointing Howard Wilkinson in 1986. So, Jock Stein's death in 1985, like the murder of Archduke Ferdinand 70 years earlier, set in place a concatenation of events which led Ferguson to Manchester M16.

The appointment of Ferguson was a seismic moment. His first interview was with Barry Davies of the BBC. Old-school interview: one on one, shirt and tie, not a water bottle, flash bulb or scarf in sight. It's well worth a proper run-out:

> Ferguson: It's excitement. Real excitement. It's a strange thing but my first and immediate reaction was 'When's the first plane?' if you know what I mean? The chairman said you have to phone Mr Edwards at Manchester United and I really, honestly ... And that's a strange thing because Aberdeen's such a great club. It's a marvellous club with a great chairman so to react that way immediately was a bit strange. I didn't expect it but that was my first thought. I couldn't possibly turn this down.
>
> Barry Davies: Yet you've been tempted before and you've been able to turn it down?
>
> Ferguson: Yeah, because, to be fair, good clubs too, but I didn't think they were above Aberdeen if you know what I mean? I didn't think they could match what's here. So many people all over Britain have a care for Manchester United. Tremendous care and concern for them and want to know how

they're doing and want to know and hope they're doing well. I hope the Manchester United players realise that responsibility and I'm sure they do. And if they do then we've got a real good chance. That's important.

Barry Davies: Do you have any feelings of sympathy for Ron Atkinson?

Ferguson: Absolutely. I said that to the players today. It's a terrible position to be in me standing there introducing myself to new players when they've lost their manager. And it's that kind of concern and they've expressed that. A lot of them are concerned for Ron Atkinson. If they have a care and concern for Ron Atkinson, the last manager, that's good. I'm glad to hear that because that gives them a real good chance. Because it is about feelings and understanding the manager is in the firing line. They'll do alright. Once we get a relationship, I'm sure we'll do very well.

It's often what's not said, isn't it? Or what is not asked? Barry Davies never asked him about when United would win the league again, nor about how he intended to break up the Merseyside hegemony. Maybe it was a deliberately gentle introduction but was it reasonably foreseeable in November 1986 that those strides would be made any time soon? The knocking Scousers off the fucking perch strides? Probably not. We were 19th in the First Division at the time, one place above the relegation zone. Ferguson oscillated between bewilderment, nervousness and anticipation; but the steel of his native Glasgow reinforced by the granite of

his adopted Aberdeen was conspicuous. His eyes narrowed
when he spoke of United players realising the responsibility
they owed to the supporters; it was clear right from the
outset, if you don't, then piss off. The proof of the pudding?
Of the 1986 squad left for Ferguson by Atkinson, all but
Bryan Robson and Clayton Blackmore were moved on in
the next five years. He was determined to rip down the
Potemkin village that Big Ron had casually put together.

I remember being pleased with the appointment. I
assumed that Ferguson, given time, would simply replicate
his Aberdeen record at United: three league titles, four FA
Cups, one League Cup, the Cup Winners' Cup and the
UEFA Super Cup. I was right and then some but as T.S.
Eliot said, 'All time is unredeemable.' And as Morrissey
said, 'How soon is now?' It might have been a case of
'bloody well get on with it' but crucially the éminence grise
of Old Trafford (Bobby Charlton) was behind Ferguson's
appointment. Only legends can buy you time. Ferguson
accepted as much in a *Mirror* football article dated 8
October 2017:

> At United, especially in the early years, I found it
> very assuring to know that Bobby was on my side.
>
> I never went out of my way to curry favour
> with him, but he had originally helped advise the
> board to sign me as a manager and I always felt he
> was in my corner.
>
> During bleak times he often said: 'You'll be all
> right. You're doing the right thing.'
>
> In the months following our 5-1 to Manchester
> City in September 1989 I was feeling a mite

vulnerable and Bobby's backing – particularly during this period – counted for a lot.

In a *Belfast Telegraph* article dated 4 July 2008 Sir Bobby explained his thoughts about the appointment at the time:

> I saw what Alex had done with Aberdeen. I saw somebody who had the nerve and the belief to go out and get what he wanted; somebody who would never be overawed by any situation. Somebody who would give the job everything that was required – and someone who also saw it as the biggest challenge in football. I have never doubted any of this since the day of his appointment, and my confidence was not harmed by the fact that I saw the old man [Busby] felt the same way.

Only legends can buy you time; two legends can buy you a bit more.

I sometimes wonder what he said to the players on the first day in training. No matter how impressive your antecedents you are always keen to please on the first day: you open doors for the contract cleaners; you overhear the receptionist on the phone to her mother and genuinely hope she recovers from her latest self-inflicted bout of gonorrhoea, syphilis and chlamydia; you fall in love with the woman who gives you keys to the filing cabinet and finds you a kettle and a few custard creams. By the time you meet your own team you have forgotten your own name. Will they know who you are? They probably will think you are Kevin Keegan given the half-gallon of Brut you ingested at 4.45 that morning. And you come out with the inanest stuff. Maybe to Bryan Robson something like this?

'Big club this, Bryan?'
    'No boss, it's a pisspot. We're shit. You should have gone to fucking Liverpool.'

But you know some blokes, don't you? Never hungover. Never miss a day. Never tired. Scratch golfers. 6am runners. Amiable wives. Can unblock a drain by just looking at it. No hot water? No problem. They can turn your brown trout tap shit into bubbling wine in no time squared. Curry from scratch. A fiery chilli? Yes, but well spiced; not just heat for heat's sake. Award-winning barbecues and lemon squash (real lemons). Shop closed? Nothing in? Whip up an omelette from a rotten marrow and a speckled grapefruit. Certificates for damson vodka. Self-assured. Know their place and value and worth. No dubiety. The easy smiling face which launched 1,000 ships of charity. Don't you just hate them? In a manunited.com podcast by Sam Carney dated 30 March 2020 Norman Whiteside shed some light on Fergie's first day:

I remember, I was injured again.
    There was only two or three of us who went to Big Ron's leaving do at his house in Rochdale. Strach [Gordon Strachan], me, Paul [McGrath] and Robbo [Bryan Robson] were there. We had a good night. A very good night.
    We came in the next morning at the gymnasium at the Cliff and Alex walks down the

stairs. He says 'I don't care who you are in this line-up here. I'm the new manager of Manchester United, my rules are my rules. I am the boss of this club now.'

He said it just like that. He actually mentioned me. He said 'I don't care if you're Whiteside, Robson or McGrath. I am the boss from hereon in.

Gordon [who played under Ferguson at Aberdeen] gave us a bit of a heads-up, [saying] he's a bit strict. You knew what you were into. New manager, you've got to adapt by the rules and get on with it. That was his intro: I'm the boss. The rest was history.

On the differences between Ferguson and his predecessor, Whiteside provided no surprises: 'Yeah, they were completely different characters. Sir Alex was always more detailed. He would have a meeting to tell you when the next meeting was! With Big Ron, you'd turn up and as long as you're fine at 3pm, you're on my team sheet.' Ferguson was above all business manager and his business was winning important trophies; he intended to do this with staggering profusion: whether the players liked him, or not, was not his concern.

It is quite revealing to examine what some of the players thought when Ferguson arrived – these were succinctly appraised in a *Daily Telegraph* article (by *Telegraph* staff and agencies) published on 4 November 2011:

Chris Turner: 'He found it extremely tough at the start. People forget that. He had to fight people at the club who were stuck in their ways a bit.'

Mike Duxbury: 'The club was not going anywhere before he arrived. I suspect it was the mentality of the players. We had a habit of playing well against big teams and losing to smaller ones, like Oxford.'

Arthur Albiston: 'His attention to detail was second to none. Ron Atkinson was more interested in the first team, but Alex restructured the club from the kids upwards.'

Graeme Hogg: 'He had the reputation of being strict and not suffering fools. We didn't know much about him, but we soon found out. I thought I started quite well, then he went and bought Steve Bruce.'

I wonder why, Graeme? I am always suspicious of players who say they are playing well: they usually end up driving lorries in Falkirk via the bench, the reserves, West Brom, Portsmouth, Hearts, Notts County and Brentford. If 999 people say it's Sunday and you say it's Monday, then unless you are a man of God you have wasted your time getting up at 7am and ironing that shirt.

Remi Moses: 'He was very professional, different than we'd had before, and that really suited me because I wasn't into drinking. He spotted certain things in my game that nobody else did.'

Peter Barnes: 'You could see he wanted to work with younger players. For one thing they were easier when it came to laying down the law.'

Paul McGrath, as revealed to Neil Moxley in a MailOnline article published on 27 February 2010:

The minute he walked in, I thought, 'I'm not going to like this' and do you know what … that's the way it worked out. I was going to flannel my way around it, but that was the truth of the matter.

But there's no doubt that if I'd have been in his position, there's no way I'd have put up with it for as long as he did. I gave him some horrendous times.

I crashed a car when I'd been out drinking. He came to see me. After a short period of abstinence, I carried on as if nothing had happened.

So where did Ferguson's rod of iron come from? Other than Apollo Creed what made him eat nails and shit thunder? Archie Knox was Ferguson's assistant at Aberdeen and United and probably knows him better than most. In an interview with *The Scotsman* published on 16 September 2017 Knox makes it clear that he regards Ferguson as the greatest:

> It all comes from his background, Govan lad, having to fight all the way, that absolute determination to succeed. And he used you guys in the press brilliantly: 'Everyone's against us, we'll never get a decision' and so on. Plus, while he and Jim McLean couldn't be separated on tactical brilliance, Alex was the better man-manager.

As Ferguson himself explained in one of his less tedious post-retirement interviews with Sarah Harris of MailOnline published on 28 February 2014 he was inspired by the life skills and moral code espoused by one of his former teachers, Elizabeth Thomson. When she passed, a keepsake was received by Ferguson from the family which sent him back to the corporal punishment days of the early

1950s: halcyon days, no doubt, when the shorts were longer, the apples greener and the chickens tastier.

> When she died, I couldn't go to the funeral because Manchester United were playing abroad, but months later I received a parcel.
>
> She had bequeathed her belt to me. Her nephew sent it to me along with a letter that said: 'You'll know more about this belt than anyone.'
>
> It's in my study. My grandchildren are terrified of it. Six from that belt and you were in absolute agony. I used to try to draw my hand away.
>
> The three ingredients to Elizabeth, when I think about it, were personality, determination and energy. Anyone who's in charge of someone else needs those three ingredients. It just won't work without them.

And what about the food as well? Shit in and shit out? I used to read Bryan Robson's articles in *Shoot!* each week about a hundred times over; I sometimes dream about them. I definitely remember his saying that Ferguson introduced fish and chicken and stopped the steak and mushrooms. In a *Sun* article by Mark Gilbert dated 24 May 2012 and entitled 'I built United on a diet of honey, toast and lemon sole', Ferguson explains the canteen revolution in his head:

> When I started as a coach – and before they started talking about diets – I used to take my team at East Stirling for lunch.

All I would give them was two slices of lemon sole, toast and honey. They used to go crazy. When I was a player, they used to give you fillet steaks and steak pie and things like that.

So when I became a manager I said to myself 'What they eat before a game is as important as what happens during the game.'

I did that at Aberdeen and I did exactly the same at United.

So maybe I am wrong about Arsène Wenger? Maybe it was lemon sole all around as far back as 1986? But sudden diet changes can precipitate a shock to the system. Some years later, I think it was Roy Keane who, on the advice of an Italian nutritionist, eschewed red meat and proteins too quickly and became ill; he missed the game at Old Trafford in October 2004 when United ended Arsenal's record unbeaten sequence: maybe the post-match pizza would have fattened him up a bit? Perhaps honey, toast and lemon sole were the reason for our performance in Fergie's first match in charge against Oxford United on Saturday, 8 November 1986, or maybe we were just plain old boiled shite?

Look at the team:

1. Chris Turner
2. Mike Duxbury
3. Arthur Albiston
4. Kevin Moran
5. Paul McGrath
6. Graeme Hogg

7. Clayton Blackmore
8. Remi Moses
9. Frank Stapleton
10. Peter Davenport
11. Peter Barnes.

It was the fabled Chinese philosopher Lao Tzu who stated: 'A journey of a thousand miles must begin with a single step.' True, but with Mike Duxbury at right-back, Graeme Hogg at centre-half, Clayton Blackmore in central midfield, Peter Davenport up front and Peter Barnes out wide it must have seemed more like a kamikaze assault on the inner core.

Of course, we lost: 2-0. David Atkinson (a lifelong Red) was there that day and according to his account detailed in a MailOnline article dated 9 May 2013 we were lucky to get the nil:

> United never looked like scoring and the two goals against were only what we deserved. United seemed tired and disinterested.
>
> Perhaps it was the famed drinking school that was rife in the club at the time? Perhaps they too were uninspired by the arrival of Fergie? But something needed to change.
>
> I was miserable leaving the stadium. I could not see how this new appointment was going to make United a better team. I'd been satisfied winning cups and, although a League title would have been special, there was something swashbuckling to me about winning big cup games and going to

Wembley, rather than grinding out results week
after week at places like Norwich.

Maybe the problem was with some of the supporters
as well? The Wembley champagne was flat and warm.
Maybe they needed honey, toast and lemon sole too? I
would have given my left ball to win away at Norwich.
Sod the FA Cup.

Act 7

Hear Me Lord

Fergie's first victory came at home to QPR on 22 November 1986: a nervy, 1-0 affair. John Sivebaek scored the winner from a free kick. This was also the first goal under Ferguson; it broke 213 barren minutes. Five words: Peter Davenport and Terry Gibson. In a BBC interview with Phil McNulty on 3 November 2011 Sivebaek (The Great Dane with the engine of Neil Webb and the vision of Mike Phelan, remember) provided some notes from a small island: 'I don't know if I deserve a place in Manchester United's history but it is nice when people remember you scored the first goal for Alex Ferguson after he arrived at the club. It is something to be proud of.'

He is right on one thing: he doesn't deserve a place in Manchester United's history apart from a footnote maybe in a special side later on ... I am convinced his signing was mistaken identity: I reckon Big Ron thought he was Michael Laudrup's brother.

And what about the hairdryer? When did that first appear? Well, as we all know, Mark Hughes's long, curly perm had disappeared to Barcelona so maybe it needed a few weeks? But everyone over the age of 18 had at least three bad long haircuts at once back in 1986, Head and Shoulders rocked, and given the piss-poor performances Ferguson was never likely to wait until Ivan Lendl and Boris Becker next gave battle. In fact, it appeared just a week after the QPR win when we lost 1-0 at Wimbledon (yes, Wimbledon) in front of 12,112 hardy souls. Peter Barnes explained the background in the *Belfast Telegraph* article dated 4 July 2008 and entitled 'Fergie's 20 years: Regime Change': 'It was there I first saw him lose his temper. He went round all the players shouting at them and telling them "You can't perform like that",' Barnes recalls. 'He said that we had to win games like that, he didn't want players who were soft. Ron was a larger-than-life personality and the players had some leeway – he didn't mind you having a drink. He was a bit sunnier than Alex, who you didn't see crack a smile too often.'

It wasn't just on the pitch and in the sanctity of the dressing room where Ferguson made his presence felt: obsessive attention to detail was also his shtick; he was the quintessential Glaswegian detective – never off duty. In the same *Belfast Telegraph* article Whiteside remembers standing in his garage after a trip to 'Costco or somewhere. I had about 100 bottles of wine and I was putting them in my wine rack,' he says. 'I had got about 88 bottles in and he [Ferguson] and Archie Knox drove past. If you went past my drive it came to a dead end, so they had to reverse quickly! He was going around seeing where his players lived.'

So, Whiteside did not get a knock on the door as Giggs and Sharpe may have got further down the line. You need to win the bread and butter battles at home before you try the tricky away fixtures. In *The Scotsman* interview from September 2017 Archie Knox was specifically asked about egos and problems:

> Maybe once, at United, there was the potential for a wee problem. I'd begun training in the morning but everyone was rubbish so I told them to go away, have a think about their attitude and come back in the afternoon, when of course footballers like to be doing their own thing.
>
> Bryan Robson went to Alex and said: 'Archie's spat out the dummy and the lads are not happy.' Alex said: 'What time does he want you back?' 'Two o'clock.' 'Then make sure you are.' So the boss backed me. If it had gone the other way I would have been beat.

It's an interesting observation isn't it? And they were as close as the walrus and Paul lost in a Glass Onion. When they arrived at United, they lived together in a shit tip somewhere in Timperley. Archie Knox explained this in an article with Tom English of *The Scotsman* published on 30 October 2011:

> A two-bedroom semi in a housing scheme. We'd never seen it before, but we took it. We went through the door, Alex dived up the stairs and got the best room and that was it.

We used to take a turn about on a Sunday morning. I'd go and get the papers and the rolls, the bacon and egg and he'd make the breakfast. I got the stuff one day and I'm in reading the paper when there's this almighty explosion. I thought the kitchen had been blown up. So I run through and here's Alex going like this, waving his arms and flapping at the fire and the smoke. There was one of these old cookers with the grill on top. He'd left a big box of these Swan matches on top of the grill and they've caught fire. What a bang! The neighbours were out and everything. 'Was that a gas explosion?' 'No, 'twas him there and a box of matches.' That could have been the end of the United thing before it got started.

We used to go to the pictures together. We'd be standing in the queue, down at that Salford Quays when it was starting to get built up and they had the big cinema thing down there and we'd go and we'd get wor sweeties and stuff like that 'cause there was nothing else to do. And people would be looking at us as if to say, 'Christ almighty, what's happening here?' I cannae mind what the pictures were. Probably fell asleep. We'd have been knackered.

Ferguson needed Archie Knox as much as he needed Bobby Charlton and Matt Busby put together. Without him he was done, and he knew it. It's odd to think that the club was in Archie Knox's hands. Who is Archie Knox? What is his story? If Archie Knox loses the players on the training field Ferguson loses the dressing room and it's a matter of time. How many other major clubs and sporting dynasties have depended on unknown midfielders from Forfar Athletic? Probably more than you think. The Nottingham Forest team of the late 70s and early 80s which won a First Division title and two European Cups was scouted, trained and coached by an ex-Coventry City goalkeeper called Peter Taylor: different town and position, same point. But what of Ferguson and Knox? Close male relationships are always intriguing, and I guess that's an important part of what football is all about too. What are the true dynamics? Where is the real source of power? Was this bromance borne out of love or plain expediency? Roy Keane made an interesting observation on this point in a MailOnline article by Rajvir Rye published on 6 October 2014 when contrasting Ferguson and Brian Clough:

> Different managers, both brilliant. I think Clough's warmth was genuine. I think with Sir Alex Ferguson it was pure business – everything is business. If he was being nice I would think: 'This is business, this.'
>
> He was driven and ruthless. That lack of warmth was his strength. United was a much bigger club than Forest but his coldness made him successful.

But do you live with someone when it's business? Cook someone breakfast when it's business? Go to the pictures with them when it's business? Wouldn't you stick them in the Travelodge and see them bright and early the next day? There has to be more to it. The pictures certainly; you have to love someone truly, madly and deeply to put up with all that throat clearing, coughing and sniffing. And that's before the popcorn, nachos, sherbet lemons and Fanta make an appearance. A labour of love worse than any mother-in-law or work-shy wife.

Ferguson managed to stabilise the club to a mid-table finish in his abridged first season; a Boxing Day win at Anfield endeared him to the United fans and made 1986 a very happy Christmas for me (as did Ian Botham's 5 for 41 against Australia at Melbourne). This victory over Liverpool on their patch must have delighted Ferguson. He was consumed with Liverpool from a very early stage; they were the benchmark. Archie Knox explained this in *The Scotsman* article dated 30 October 2011:

> There was a discipline problem at the club. Boys drinking and drink-driving. Always stories about us. Always leaks from the dressing room. Well, that had to stop for a start. And it did stop. We stopped it dead. Players were doing similar things at Anfield, but nothing ever came out of there. Never one iota came out of that club. Alex was constantly on about that. Whatever goes on here it doesn't leave here. It stays where it is. He became a little bit obsessed with Liverpool. I can remember going to Liverpool, maybe our first time there, and after the match there's Kenny [Dalglish] and Joe Fagan and Ronnie Moran and Roy Evans and the whole backroom staff, scouts and everything piled in and Alex and I went in on our own and it was

'Aye, your team played well today.' I can't remember the score; 2-1 to them or something like that, and it was that sort of patronising way they had. Alex walks out the door and says, 'Right, that'll be the last time we'll be in there on our own.' Next season we went in mob-handed. Everybody's there, the reserve team coach, youth team coach, kit man, laundry lady, girls who make the tea. We were all in the room. Alex didn't want them intimidating us with their numbers.

This was an era before the European Commission started to piss its rotten aubergines and fresh fish on our game. With no transfer window restrictions in place Ferguson could have waved the cheque book. It is perhaps surprising that he waited until the summer to reinforce. Look at that Oxford line-up again? I mean, come on! Could you have had Chris Turner in goal for 23 games? Who knows, a few January buys and we might have strung together a cup run? Well, we did until Coventry City beat us at home in the fourth round. People talk about Ferguson's temper and hair trigger, but he knew he needed to make the right moves and not dive in. His first signing was the England right-back Viv Anderson who had won the First Division and two European Cups with Nottingham Forest; no one could argue with that: certainly not Mike Duxbury. I was really happy with Brian McClair as well: by now the middle-class Magill juggernaut had chugged its way towards the log cabins and chalets of Scotland in October half-term. Fluffy-looking blokes in skirts serving you brunch and calling you sir. More importantly, we got the Scottish

League Cup Final live. McClair scored for Celtic in that 1986 final and that was enough for me. I still thought goals in Scotland meant goals in England. But what of Liverpool? They had sold Ian Rush to Juventus but with the money they bought John Barnes, Peter Beardsley and John Aldridge. It's bloody typical isn't it? Just as Athens takes a nap Rome discovers its spatha and pila.

I procured a paper round in the summer of 1987. The *Warrington Mercury*. I got a tenner a week for delivering about 500 papers. That was money well earned – 2p a paper. I could live with that but the rabid dogs baying for blood in the driveway? That was a bit much. The old fellas could go one of two ways. Either they would tell you to 'fuck off and never come back again' decrying 'how they did not fight a war for this kind of journalistic free speech' or they would invite you inside for a Wagon Wheel and an undiluted Vimto and ask you if algebra was still on the maths syllabus these days. So, what was I getting paid coppers and risking rabies and hookworm for? Go on, have a guess. Julie Black? I mentioned her earlier. The one I shared Hula Hoops and chips with the summer before? Well, I spent £3 of my first wage packet on a box of Terry's All Gold for her. Don't worry I've already done the maths: that's 150 papers and enough diseased mutts and ditch-water conversation to be thoroughly pissed off when she never talked to me again after I left said chocolates at her porch. The ingratitude. It just fired my zeal for football and every other penny I earned that summer holiday (about 57 quid) went into my NatWest savers account. You remember the pig one? I got Woody, Annabel and (when I hit 50 notes) big brother Maxwell. I would also have obtained ten per cent interest in halcyon days for savers if I hadn't earmarked the money for a swift withdrawal or four: it was the United fund. At least they couldn't take the ceramic pigs back.

I started to hang out a bit more with David Flynn. He had moved on from The Beatles and Bob Dylan into The Smiths. I thought The Smiths were the square crisps in city-blue packets that appeared all too infrequently in our house or the salt in the bag merchants who sponsored England schoolboys. What a stupid idea. Salt your own crisps. Mind you, I know such tramps who shovel in their own vinegar too. When he started humming 'Heaven Knows I'm Miserable Now' I just assumed it was a stream of consciousness thing about Terry Gibson and Graeme Hogg. Of course, I joined in. So Flynny has this idea about us two going to Old Trafford on our own. Like a seasoned quantity surveyor he has it all worked out to the nearest bolt and welly: £1.20 half return to Trafford Park from Warrington Central, £1.40 to stand on the Stretford End, a quid for pie and chips at Lou Macari's, 50p for a programme, 90p change from a fiver for hamburger and chips in McDonald's in town once we got back. What a day. I said yes straight away. The 57 nicker or so would mean ten games alone and what with Christmas money it could even be 11! I could keep doing the paper round. Let's just get season tickets. Might be cheaper in the long run? How about some away games as well? Where exactly is Portsmouth? How many programme tokens do we need to get to Wembley?

It's funny how you always get carried away in the warm bath of a good idea or result: it's a totally elastic concept which age does not wither. Your law firm has one exploratory meeting with an agent for pop stars' and footballers' mis-sold tax schemes and the owners leave convinced that one letter to the offending financial adviser will lead to riches: the firm will be sold for £50 million by Maundy Thursday and it will be burgers and beers with Whoopi Goldberg by Whitsun. Of course, the agent knows the glitterati only in his own glossy mind; before the Robinsons Barley Water is served at Wimbledon the receivers have rampaged their way through the extension leads and footrests and left a used tea bag behind. And you are left depressed and unemployed, partying like it's 2002 with just ITV3 and Arthur Daley for company for the next six months. While these guys had no excuse, we did: the first game Flynny and I earmarked for this jamboree was Watford: Saturday, 22 August 1987.

But what would I tell Dad? I wasn't allowed to the disco at Grappenhall Sports club that summer and that was only down the bloody road; I wasn't even allowed to Walton Gardens to pitch and putt when it was raining: someone had daubed the bandstand with tasty graffiti about Sally Slater and clap but it wasn't me. I didn't even like the girl. So, what chance Old Trafford? But help was at hand in the unlikely form of the British Elvis Presley. Seriously. A few weeks earlier Sir Cliff had visited Warrington to play some soft tennis indoors (it was pissing it down, of course) and I battled my way through the intense competition of the North West's finest Under 12s serve-and-volley merchants to play one game with a man I had never heard of. Was he in the Beatles? I remember his Persil white tennis outfit stood out amongst the assorted football strips and Adidas joggers of our lot, and how tanned he was. But, again, it's all relative: the damp summer had accentuated the wan complexion almost guaranteed by a diet that loathed Mediterranean colour and never strayed too far from the holy trinity of Findus Crispy Pancakes, oven chips and Butterscotch Angel Delight. I can't even remember if I did defeat Sir Cliff. I do remember thinking why is he playing with his glasses on? Anyway, after the game he shook my hand heartily, said I'd be a great tennis player (there again he said he'd make it in the States) and then presented me with a Donnay tennis bag and lessons with a local coach. What good is a tennis bag with no bloody racket in it? There was no way I was going to lessons with the square-wheeled, wooden, John McEnroe effort that went out with the ark.

John White was the coach although he was nicknamed Chalky because of chalk lines in tennis. If that passed for funny, I was out. I had no intention of going anyway so this was my excuse all those Saturday afternoons: I was learning how to chip and charge and slice a backhand with Chalky White. It was never questioned because you don't question Sir Cliff, do you? You don't question a national treasure. I still had no cash card for the hole in the wall, so I had to draw out my fiver in the bank that morning. I felt dirty and treacherous, as if I was robbing the place. The look of disappointment in the assistant manager's eyes almost made me change my mind (for the first time ever he didn't even ask me if I wanted a statement), but there comes a time in every boy's life when he must feed the birds instead. I met Flynny at Bullough's Sports in Stockton Heath that day and we walked the couple of miles to town

– the tennis bag held me down a bit but there you go. Anything for the love of the game. The 1.10pm train got us to Trafford Park by 1.30. From there we followed the red, white and black scarves to the chippy and the ground amidst the excitement and humour bubbles of the day. 'Look at that daft cunt with the tennis bag. Where's your fucking headband, Boris?' We hit Old Trafford about 2pm. Stretford End bound. Conscious of seeing next to nothing a few years earlier I made a beeline for the front railings. I could see the boys limbering up: I could hear Robson jokingly telling McClair he was 'fucking wank' when he failed to hit the crossbar from 20 yards or so. The Stretford End had a song for each favourite.

'He's here. He's there. He's every fucking where. That's Brian McClair. That's Brian McClair.'

I can't quite remember the chords or the melody to Mike Duxbury's. Or the lyrics for that matter. This aside, the team was slowly being transformed into the personality of its manager:

1. Gary Walsh
2. Viv Anderson
3. Mike Duxbury
4. Remi Moses
5. Paul McGrath
6. Kevin Moran
7. Bryan Robson (captain)
8. Gordon Strachan
9. Brian McClair
10. Norman Whiteside
11. Jesper Olsen.

A 2-0 win and McClair scored his first United goal at the Stretford End in front of me. I can hear his roar now. It was a great day that; Trafford Park was a lot harder to get back to mind. Lucky Flynny was a cricket fan as well. He knew that Warwick Road station was next to the nearby cricket ground and would get us back to Oxford Road unless we got the wrong platform and ended up in Altrincham; we were home by 6.30 and the tennis bag was in the garage with the match programme.

Word was catching on about the exploits of Messrs Flynn and Magill. He was a dude already, so it did my reputation no harm. Tony Pucill wanted to join us, amongst others, for the next adventure which would be against Newcastle a few weeks later. We were second years at big school now (which is probably year 157 in today's nonsense vernacular) and we had just amalgamated with the other big comprehensive in the village, so everything was on a larger scale. The bullshit, for example. Tony pulled out of the Newcastle trip at the last minute as he had been personally invited by Bryan Robson to travel to the ground with the team on the coach; Robson was hoping Tony would sign for United as he was the best 12-year-old footballer in England, a view not shared by the sports master at Bridgewater High who never selected him. But Tony would not be tied down. It could be angling or something international: he relieved the Bridgewater Canal of four million mirror carp that summer and his parents owned Ewing Oil following a hostile takeover which left J.R. and Bobby at loggerheads. We drew against Newcastle. Flynny and I blamed it on the Stretford Paddock which we opted for that day. Never again. On

Monday Tony asked us if we saw him on the pitch at half-time replacing divots and draining the goalmouth with his pitchfork.

Liverpool were unstoppable that season. John Barnes in particular was sublime. Bizarre as it sounds Liverpool did not miss Ian Rush; in fact they were better: they did not need to rely on a more direct style of play and the coruscating pace of Rush; they had flair out wide now and the dazzling quality of Peter Beardsley dropping into midfield. That 1987/88 Liverpool side was one of the best English club sides. Yet we were more than a match for them when we met on Sunday, 15 November 1987, live on ITV. Aldridge put Liverpool ahead, Whiteside equalised and thereafter Liverpool were clinging on in the torrential rain; I can remember saying to my dad: 'Liverpool aren't better than United, they're just more consistent.' He somnolently nodded and retreated to his Stones Bitter – strong stuff that. Only four days earlier England (including Robson, Barnes and Beardsley) had travelled to Yugoslavia for an enervating European Championship qualifier; no doubt the rest of the players on show that Sunday had clocked up air miles that midweek too. You would not have known. A terrific game of pace, energy and quality: an eloquent example of the utter futility of the international break.

It was a battle for second alright and by Boxing Day we were in the hunt and still in the cups. Steve Bruce was on the way too that Christmas: a solid central-defensive partner for Paul McGrath to replace the ageing Kevin Moran. Like Hai Karate aftershave, not a bad Christmas gift as long as we snaffled the cold turkey and pickles on offer at St James' Park. Did we ding. And it had something to do with a midfield player called Paul Gascoigne.

In a *Daily Telegraph* article by Giles Mole dated 3 June 2008 Ferguson recalled the game:

> Around 1987, when Newcastle were bobbing above the relegation zone, we played them and my three central midfielders that day were Bryan Robson, Norman Whiteside and Remi Moses. All great footballers and he just tore them apart.
>
> When he nutmegged Moses and patted him on the head, I was out of the dugout shouting 'Get that f****** so-and-so'.
>
> Robbo and Whiteside were chasing him up and down the pitch and they couldn't get near him.

Ryan Giggs recently revealed four players who never received the hairdryer treatment: Cantona, Keane, Robson and Ronaldo. But Giggs started in 1991, not in 1986; I often wonder whether Robson got a blast early doors. If he did, it was probably this day. How would he have reacted? Context and attention to detail is everything. Robson hailed from Chester-le-Street and was a boyhood Newcastle fan so his family may well have been there, especially as this was the festive period. You know the drill: it's all snowballs and stockings on Christmas Eve but by Boxing Day you are ready to murder each other so it's either the nick, the pantomime with Little and Large and Bella Emberg or the football. When you know you've played badly and a kid is taking you to school in front of your folks you are unlikely to unload; I think something slightly sterile along the lines of: 'Boss? Do you think I really wanna play bad in front of me Mam and Dad?' In a *Daily Star* interview with Paul Brown dated 9 May 2013 Robson explained his feelings when the hairdryer first appeared:

> I did think it was weird, the first time he attacked Paul McGrath with the hairdryer. You just had to hide your head because you'd start laughing that it wasn't you!
>
> The boss was giving him a b*****king for seeing him do something in the game he wasn't happy about.

McGrath could have been just as good as Robson. Maybe even better. If he got it, I'm sure Robson did as well. There is something wonderfully fair-minded about the true autocrats.

And so, while the opportunity of silverware knocked only in the cup competitions, you sensed this was different from the bloated days of Big Ron. Our league form was consistent; we had a solid back four reinforced by Viv Anderson and Steve Bruce and Brian McClair would become the first United player in 20 years (since George Best in fact) to break the 20 league goals barrier. Steve Bruce is an interesting one: apparently United had Terry Butcher lined up until he broke his leg playing for Rangers the month before. With a simple twist of fate Bruce would become a proper United legend when he might have remained a solid stopper at Norwich City. I was at Old Trafford for one of the early League Cup rounds against Bury courtesy of Tony Pucill's dad who agreed to take us. 'Jamie, don't mention Ewing Oil in the car. Dad's had to sign a non-disclosure agreement with the CIA and it's all a bit up in the air. He's flying to Texas in the morning to meet Larry Hagman and Patrick Duffy.' We stopped for chilli dogs on the way there and chips and chop suey rolls on the way back. His dad was some bloke to do that under all that pressure. And how well he was coping with the news that all the cortisone injections administered by the United medical team had effectively shattered his son's knee and footballing dreams. My dad had no stress at all, and you wouldn't get a sugar sandwich out of him.

This took us to the quarter-finals where we played Oxford United at the Manor Ground. Liverpool had already been vanquished so why not? An early trophy for Ferguson would settle things down a bit. It was a proper trophy too back then when more than a bit of water separated us from Europe. Why is it that a shit ground not fit for purpose is always described as 'tight and compact'? Or 'atmospheric'? Why is it said that 'the players will relish the fans being so close to the pitch' when clearly, they will hate every foul-mouthed, spitballed moment? Oxford had lost six of the previous seven. Not for the first time in the League Cup we struggled at that tight and compact little ground; 2-0 down at half-time. Upon the restart Barry Davies in his BBC commentary remarked: 'Manchester United surely in need of a supreme performance in the second period if their season is not to be reduced to one competition.' The date? It was 20 January 1988. Final score: Oxford United 2 Manchester United 0. What was it about Oxford United and the League Cup?

Barry Davies did not waste his words. This was the leitmotif of United in the 1980s: it's January and we are one game away from shit or bust.

This would arrive the following month in an FA Cup fifth-round tie against Arsenal at Highbury. It had that 'tie of the round' feel to it although I am sure Port Vale and Watford felt the same way. In the 87th minute, at 2-1 down Whiteside is bundled over by Michael Thomas and a very dubious penalty is given. I'd like to say 'I've seen them given, Brian' but in front of the North Bank? I don't think I have; only before the Anfield Kop or Ivan the Terrible was such largesse for visiting opponents less likely to be afforded. Over to Brian Moore at ITV:

> Oh! He's missed it! What a mistake! Alec Ferguson, the manager, with his head in his hands. And a glorious, glorious opportunity for United is celebrated there on the North Bank and a kick that is sent sailing over the Arsenal crossbar. And perhaps the last chance for United is gone for Brian McClair.

And that was that. Mike Duxbury's own goal wins it for Arsenal (I'm saying nothing). It is safe to say that every trace of Brian McClair was removed from my bedroom walls that cold night in February 1988. It was a bad row. Was it me? Or was it him? Did we want the same thing? Could either of us change? Were the differences irreconcilable? Surely his behaviour was unreasonable? After watching the highlights, I reached a salty-eyed conclusion: I would initiate divorce proceedings on

Monday morning. On Tuesday night McClair scored away at Tottenham; the solicitors were stood down and we were back on. Well before the days of snakebite and green pints and bar prices in Braille I knew that Saturday nights were not good for relationships: say nothing and wait until the morning, Jamie. Unfortunately, saying and doing are not the same thing.

League performance is the true measure of improvement and evolution. In Ferguson's first truncated season we finished 11th on 56 points; this time we finished second with 81 points. This was tangible progress. The Easter Monday game against the champions-elect at Anfield confirmed this: 3-1 down, outplayed, outclassed, outmanoeuvred; yet we came back to draw deservedly. Gordon Strachan's faux cigar-smoking celebration in front of the Kop upon scoring the equaliser made us piss as much as it made them itch. Then we have Norman Whiteside who within minutes of entering the fray had already elbowed Barnes and savagely raked McMahon. The point? We were not prepared to be intimidated. Would we have done this under Big Ron? Or would it have been a light ale and a laugh with Kenny and his staff in the Boot Room? Ferguson was far from done after the game: he was determined to leave Liverpool with his own score draw. As recalled by Steven Pye in a *Guardian* sports article dated 13 December 2018:

> I can now understand why teams come away from here choking on their own vomit and biting their tongues knowing they have been done by the referee. I'm not getting at this referee. The

whole intimidating atmosphere and the monopoly Liverpool have enjoyed for years gets to them eventually.

Dalglish on hearing Ferguson's remarks during a radio interview when carrying his six-week-old daughter spat the dummy: 'You might as well talk to my daughter,' Dalglish said. 'You will get more sense out of her.'

A score draw maybe. But this one was far from over.

Flynny and I went to ten home games that season. We were getting that swagger about us before it became popularised: our jeans were a bit baggier than the Warrington boys were comfortable with; we rocked the tracksuit-top look which drew some odd glances at home. Terrace fashion was making a mark. Oh, and we were a keeper, a midfielder and striker away from an excellent side.

Act 8

I Live For You

Two of the missing three pieces arrived in the summer of 1988 dominated by Bros, the West Indies pacemen and England's woeful performance at the Euros. Jim Leighton was, at the time (Shilton and Southall excepted), generally regarded as Britain's best keeper: a custodian of the Aberdeen side which conquered the Old Firm and the continent; a veteran of World Cup finals. A solid reputation. A safe pair of hands. Well? You would go on a bit after two seasons of Chris Turner. Mark Hughes was back as well following spells at Barcelona and Bayern Munich. Hughes seemed a perfect foil for McClair: his physical presence and ability to hold up the ball would naturally complement McClair's busy style of pace and movement.

As for the final piece? A central midfielder? Ferguson famously thought he had clinched the signature of Paul Gascoigne only to be told while on holiday that Terry Venables had stolen a march, or, more accurately, bought his parents a house. As Ferguson explained in a *Mirror* article

by Mike Walters on 3 June 2008, missing out on Gazza
was the biggest regret of his Manchester United career:

> Alan Shearer was one, but for me the most
> disappointing of all was Paul Gascoigne. He was
> the best player of his era, a breath of fresh air
> because he played with a smile.
>
> We spoke to him and the night before I went
> on holiday, he says, 'Go and enjoy yourself, Mr
> Ferguson, I'll be signing for Manchester United.'
>
> So I went on my holidays but Martin Edwards
> (then chairman) rang and said 'I've got some bad
> news – he signed for Tottenham. They bought a
> house for his mother and father in the north east
> and that swung it.'
>
> I think it was a bad mistake, and Paul admits it.
>
> We had Bryan Robson, a Geordie. Steve Bruce,
> a Geordie. Gary Pallister, from Middlesbrough …
> we had a structure of players who could have helped
> him and it could have given him some discipline.

A regret shared by Gascoigne himself as he explained in a
BT Sport interview with Darren Fletcher in February 2015:

> It was my family's fault. I was on the way there
> to sign for Man United. I remember saying to Sir
> Alex 'You're going on holiday so I'm going to sign
> for the club.' On the way there I got a call from
> Spurs. They said my family had nothing when I
> was growing up but if I went there they'd buy my
> mum and dad a house.

So I went 'Dad, Spurs said they're going to buy you a house.' He said 'well what are you waiting for?' So I said to Spurs that I would sign. Then my sister called and said 'Paul, if Mum and Dad are getting a house, I want a sunbed.' So I signed for the club, and when you sign you get fan mail. The first letter was from Sir Alex Ferguson. It wasn't a good letter. I got caned. He was like 'I can't believe you turned down the biggest club.'

You know, sometimes, I do look back and think about what would have been if, what would I have won at Man United? When I signed for Spurs, Man United weren't winning everything, but then all the young kids came through and they started winning everything. It's probably one of the regrets I have.

Gascoigne would have added class and personality to the steel and drive of Bryan Robson; the fans would have adored him. So why not buy his parents a house in the bloody North East then? You could have snapped up a four-bedroom detached house in Newcastle for 80 odd grand back then and bought the whole of Sunderland with the change. And what did we do instead? Well, just a few months later in November 1988 we bought Ralph Milne for £170,000, a signing Ferguson later regarded as his worst ever. It's not a hindsight thing either. When you pay that kind of fee to a Third Division side (Bristol City) for a 27-year-old player who has not played for Scotland then you know at the time what's going to happen; you don't need Teletext or Neil Kinnock to tell you. It's an odd thing revisionism: people now think Fergie never lost a game; they also think he never bought a shit player. Not true; nor was it all champagne football either. As for Gazza? You are only ready when you are ready. And that goes for anything in life: drink, career, relationships, maturity. And he was nowhere near ready. If you are not ready the hammer will be as ineffective as the velvet glove. Anyone thinking that Ferguson's discipline or a roast dinner at Robson's would have helped is plain wrong; it goes much deeper than clichés and onion gravy I'm afraid. What about George Best? Did Sir Matt sort him out? Did Sir Bobby and Denis Law? Best wasn't ready either; it's the same thing. People forget that footballers have their own lives and families; they also assume just because you play for the same club that you are all bosom buddies. So that lady in accounts with the annoying cough and perpetual sniffle who is struggling to adapt to life in London after moving from Scunthorpe? Would you let her have your spare room?

The first game of the 1988/89 campaign was at home to QPR. The team was solid, embossed with Ferguson's personality like a company seal:

1. Jim Leighton
2. Clayton Blackmore
3. Lee Martin
4. Steve Bruce
5. Paul McGrath
6. Brian McClair
7. Bryan Robson (captain)
8. Gordon Strachan

9. Peter Davenport
10. Mark Hughes
11. Jesper Olsen.

OK, well maybe not quite a team in the manager's mould. Clayton Blackmore? We called him 'The Heater' as he kept Bryan Robson's shirt warm, but this was no excuse for him wearing every other bloody jersey as well. Replace The Heater with 'The Spider' (Viv Anderson, who must have been injured), Davenport with Gascoigne and it looks like this:

1. Jim Leighton
2. Viv Anderson
3. Lee Martin
4. Steve Bruce
5. Paul McGrath
6. Paul Gascoigne
7. Bryan Robson (captain)
8. Gordon Strachan
9. Brian McClair
10. Mark Hughes
11. Jesper Olsen.

That side would have won the title in 1988/89. I have no doubt. No one remembers either some of Ferguson's more bizarre team selections; for example, McClair must have played in midfield in this game. So, this fella scores 24 league goals the previous season, you pay a club record £1.8m for Mark Hughes to partner him and then you stick him in midfield and start with Peter Davenport up top. Madness! Imagine how Martin Edwards must have felt? He has put his financial balls through the mincer of sleepless nights for this and he gets Peter Davenport in return? I felt a bit sorry for some of the chairmen back then. Football had a slightly different rule of law. If you ran a typing department in 1988 and you asked the director for 37 Apple word processors at significant cost, how would he react when he saw they were gathering dust and the secretaries were still hacking away? All blood, broken nails and Tippex at the ready. You'd be looking for another bloody job.

When I wasn't at United with Flynny, Saturday afternoons would follow a similar pattern. Fortified by a morning trip into town to buy nothing with nothing and watch the girls go by (or *Going Live!* and *Saint and Greavsie* if it was raining), I would watch Dad's team play at Belvoir Road. They had two teams so generally one of them would be at home. We now lived close by too so if you got there about 2.30 you had half an hour to kick into the nets before the fat bastards emerged from the dressing rooms to tell you to 'fuck off out of the fucking goalmouth'. You could reconstruct old games with that wonderful under-the-breath commentary and pretend you were Brian McClair at the same time, if he wasn't playing in midfield. The trouble was that most other kids had the same idea. The older ones. The bigger ones. The harder ones. Like Kennedy Dikes. He had already won the gold swimming survival badge and certificate: 64 lengths in a snorkel parka and Wrangler drainpipes is not to be messed with. Especially when he has picked up a rubber brick from the deep end. We called him 'De-icer' but not to his face.

By about 2.35pm your ball would have been gleefully volleyed into Runcorn. They would let you join in the headers and volleys games after kick-off on the smaller pitch as long as you were in goal and collected the ball. It wasn't all one-way traffic: when De-icer went in for a drink one day, we stole his ball and ran off. It was well worth a beating to imagine the look on his face and tell him to 'fuck off' when he rang up asking for it back. He also once got booted by the opposition keeper for rolling the ball up his net during the match. He got threatened with 'ten tonne of steel toecap 'up his arse a number of times but there is no one as blind as he that won't listen. I can hear the thwack now! Fully deserved.

This was the routine back then which had a kind of bucolic consistency. So, it came as a shock when my dad and a few of his pals took me for a drive on the lunchtime of the QPR game. I hardly knew them; they arrived for a barbecue or a casserole now and then and asked about your geography homework on the landing, but you never took part. You were sent to your room with a bag of Chipsticks while they talked about luncheon vouchers and timeshares over shit percolated coffee no one liked but everyone pretended to enjoy. As we moved towards Lou Macari's chippy on Chester Road it dawned on me that this was United-related – the throngs of people in red and black and white gave it away; you can always tell those eagle-eyed beavers destined for a career in law. Only as we trundled into the private car park with men in brass buttons saluting us did I conclude that there was something faintly nouveau riche about all this. Dad worked at a brewery and we were guests of Guinness in their executive box. He loved it all. He had arrived.

First thought? The box was bloody small and there were too many people in it for us all to see the game through the tiny window. To mitigate this and to celebrate Mark Hughes's return I sharpened the elbows and marked my ground. I needn't have bothered: they were talking transport planning and distribution over lashings of black velvet; I was the only one watching the green stuff. The box was essentially soundproof so no atmosphere; when there were a few muffled cheers or gasps there was a gargantuan TV in the box (much bigger than the width of the window) for an immediate replay. When the steaks arrived, they all disappeared to the restaurant and I was the lone inhabitant. I asked for my steak 'well done' because everyone asked for their steak well done in 1988. There was no other way. We were so far away from the pitch that the players looked Lilliputian but it was clear that Paul Parker had Mark Hughes in his back pocket. I wished I was with Flynny kicking every ball, not part of this deep-fried, sautéed circus. The Guinness fella came in half-cut and announced in James Joyce style that 'Jim Leighton has fucking chicken legs' and then disappeared. Thanks for that mate. And the 0-0. I could have made a difference out there.

And it was my first experience of the pissed talk of three or four blokes on the way back home. My dad was a big fan of the declamatory speech on any form of occasion, so I was somewhere between the danger zone and the eye of a hurricane. It was words along the lines of 'This next ten years will make or break you, Jamie.' 'Work hard and this could be you every fortnight.' 'Guinness and steak.' He was that pissed he started to give me his luncheon vouchers and petrol tokens. Well, I think every dad of the 1980s tried to place their sons in the prison of a good job. They meant no harm, but did they? Had they not read George Orwell? Did they not realise that Gordon Comstock wanted to write not work as an advertising executive? Why should they benefit from their own literary ignorance? The ones who had it right were working that Saturday afternoon for themselves. Not waiting for the sack when the share price goes south, and the steaks dry up.

Flynny was a proper fan but it's easier to be a proper fan when your stepdad is an affable man with cash to burn and a Cortina Crusader in his drive. He was a self-employed hairdresser with no interest in the middle-class journey. Therefore he could afford his house (none of this 'buy the cheapest house on the best street nearest to the highest ranking school and swim 20 fathoms deep in mortgage debt bullshit'), he didn't take the kids abroad purely to show off to his friends, he had no university fund to further dry up the happiness of cash flow either and he was a cool guy too. Bob Dylan, The Beatles, The Stone Roses, proper Coca-Cola and Mars bars all round. And why not? The problem with deferred gratification is that it almost never arrives and when it does it is either shit or not what you expected. And what's the point in that? Enduring life rather than enjoying it? If you are not enjoying reading this then you will put it down and put those shelves up for your wife or drive your mother-in-law to Betws-y-Coed for the tea and bara brith you promised her back in 1993. But you won't. Will you?

You know what you get with a Mars bar and a season ticket. Flynny decided on United Road. It was a bit tastier

and harder core than the Stretford End and more away
supporters tried to infiltrate it; hot spots of trouble broke
out intermittently, so it was christened 'The Animal House'.
I'm not sure how much he paid for a season ticket but one
thing it did do was make him an automatic United club
member and pretty much guarantee him away tickets and
a place on the coach. He had even joined the Warrington
supporters' branch. This also meant that he could vouch
for me if I paid three quid to be a member, which I did.
Membership was otherwise ineffably futile. You could visit
the Old Trafford museum? But you would be disturbing
the dust on the bowl of leaves of what exactly? The rose
leaves of league championships we did not have? You don't
want to be reminded of certain things. Luckily in the good
old-fashioned tradition of Mancunian customer care it was
closed on matchdays.

My tennis was still being used as the matchday excuse.
I nearly got rumbled in Crete in 1988 when we entered
a tournament of sorts against some Germans staying at
the same hotel. Dad was extremely confident we would
win with Cliff Richard and a year's experience on our
side. I was double shit but blamed the clay surface. I had
trained on a hard court you see. You can't expect Novak
to beat Rafa on clay, can you? We chose Goodison Park
for our first away trip: Sunday, 30 October 1988. It all fell
neatly into place. Flynny made all the arrangements. In
the days where BT payphones were literally currency, he
would ghost in looking all inconspicuous with his Flying
Squad duffel coat and half-eaten meat and potato pie; a
touch of legerdemain and a few digits later and something
like 400 quid would appear as a credit. So he was on

the phone to the United club line (and lots more prurient things besides) 24/7: luckily Stockton Heath only had one PC and he couldn't catch a snake or a ladder in a convalescent home. We had no club game that weekend either (though plenty of annoying midweek night games early in the season) and it was half-term the day after so no school to bollocks it all up. So it would be easy to say that tennis had been switched to Sunday because of the holidays and I'm watching a video with Flynny after and would be back around nine; this gave us ample time to discard the false noses and moustaches and get back from Liverpool.

Dad called Flynn's stepdad who knew the score and kept ice-cool under pressure. We got on the coach around 1pm at Goodies in Warrington with a load of other United-mad lads. It was surprising the driver could see with the miasma of Embassy Number 1 all around; I'd never seen so much lager either. Fuck it! I had a couple. I tried to join in the raucous singing, but even then I was a man of chords and melody; I needed time with the lyrics. Put it this way: it wasn't 'Abide With Me'.

We disembarked about 100 miles from the ground with a Scouse police escort hissing and spitting at us. So, the police play fair all the time, do they? Not here they didn't. There were plenty of sly digs and rabbit punches at the 'fucking Manc scum'. Do you think if I mentioned I wasn't a Manc it would have made any difference? I just thought it was Liverpool that hated us. But it was Everton as well, so I hated them back straight away. We were stood in the tiny pen behind one of the goals, but I was finding my sea legs by now:

Hello, Hello!
We are the Busby Boys
Hello, Hello!
We are the Busby Boys
And if you're a Scouser, surrender or die
Cos we all follow United
U-N-I-T-E-D
United are the team for me
With a knick knack paddy whack
Give a dog a bone
All you Scousers fuck off home.

Hughes scored first with a brilliant volley in front of us. I had never heard such an infernal din. In the pandemonium which ensued, the dominoes of supporters behind us collapsed and Flynny and I were catapulted about that tiny terrace like rag dolls. He ended up near the front with smashed-up ribs. He didn't care one bit; he probably enjoyed it: a war wound which would sew a deeper narrative of love and belonging. I practised songs with him on the walk back to the coach and joined in the below with something bordering on confidence:

United flag is deepest red
It shrouded all our Munich dead.
Before their limbs grew stiff and cold
Their heart blood dyed its every fold
Then raise United's banner high
Beneath its shade we'll live and die
So keep the faith and never fear
We'll keep the red flag flying here

We'll never die, we'll never die
We'll never die, we'll never die
We'll keep the red flag flying high
'cause Man United will never die.

We arrived back at Goodies and Flynny's dad picked us up. 'Good game that,' he said. 'United should have been out of sight.' 'How the fuck do you know?' I asked. 'It was on the TV you dick.'

Oh, fucking hell! I had no idea it was the live game. I was now three-parts convinced that Dad had seen my cavorting behind the goal, and I would never be allowed out again. What a day to wear that fluorescent yellow Nike cap! I slung it out of the window: there was nothing else I could do. A few months later he asked about the cap but not where I was that late autumn afternoon in 1988.

What is worse? New Year's Day or New Year's Eve? The latter confirms you are not a loner by choice; the former that you have nothing to look forward to – it's a tough one. In 1989 it was definitely New Year's Day: United v Liverpool live on ITV. It was normal service on 70 minutes when Barnes put Liverpool ahead but three goals in six minutes from McClair, Hughes and Beardsmore gave us an unlikely win. Maybe there was something to look forward to after all? Russell Beardsmore was a homegrown young lad; he played quite well that day – Mark Robins, Billy Garton, Deiniol Graham and Tony Gill were waiting in the wings. We had also bought a floppy-haired, fresh-faced 17-year-old with a sweet foot called Lee Sharpe from Torquay United the previous June. These were somewhat predictably called 'Fergie's Fledglings'. That hysteria lasted less than 24 hours:

we lost 1-0 at Middlesbrough the very next day. Maybe, like Icarus, they had read the papers and flown too close to the Ayresome Park mud? It's not as daft as it sounds: no one had heard of fixture congestion back then.

It was then headlines of the wrong sort. Problems persisted with Whiteside and McGrath. As McGrath revealed in an interview with Donald McRae of *The Guardian* on 24 October 2006:

> We were on a collision course, me and Alex, because he was out to seize control of the club by barking at everyone. He had me and Norman in the office all the time, shouting and fining us, but it didn't work. We were injured a lot of the time and we'd be at a loss after rehabilitation work in the morning, so inevitably we'd end up on a bar-stool in the afternoon saying, 'Aw, let's just go for it.'
>
> I'd had lots of knee operations by then and Alex thought, 'Hang on, this is a drinker with rotten knees ... ' He was right and, if I'd been him, I'd have kicked me and Norman out a long time before then.

It was around this time that McGrath and Whiteside appeared on Granada TV's *Kick Off* show looking on the wasted side of well-oiled. When McGrath was asked how much he had before the show, in a one-on-one article with Sam Pilger dated 1 January 2007:

> It was more like a few dozen. We had a lot that day. Norman had asked me to go on this programme

with him on a Friday afternoon before a game. I was
nervous about doing live television, but decided this
should be my first go at it. To settle my nerves we
went to The Trafford and had a skinful. I had even
more than Norman, and overdid it to say the least.

Neither of them would see out 1989 as United players.

Forest knocked us out of the FA Cup in March.
Attendances dwindled thereafter as we plummeted down
the unforgiving rocks of the First Division. This was the
start of the deepest, darkest days for Ferguson: Gordon
Strachan was sold when we desperately needed his quality
and attacking intent. Sold to Leeds as well? Did Ferguson
not know we hated them? Had no one told him? Did he
not read the history books? Or ask Sir Bobby? You do not
sell to Leeds unless you are selling them shit. There is
mutual respect between United and Liverpool but none
between United and Leeds. Is it to do with Richard of
York giving battle in vain at Bosworth Field? Henry VII's
draconian tax laws? The Pennines? Mike Atherton's cover
drive? James Milner? Fish and chips? Sticks of rock? Sugar
dummies? No. We have no respect for them because they
have won next to nothing and they hate us for a good day
out. At least Liverpool fans go to Blackpool for their fish
and chips and support Lancashire in the cricket.

Ferguson was later eulogised for his man-management
style but maybe the 1989 version needed as much work
as the team and the stadium? Strachan set out his views
in a *Daily Record* article entitled 'Fergie treated me like a
child' which was reproduced in the redcafe.net forum on
31 July 2006:

United's Gary Bailey denies Gordon Smith and Brighton and Hove Albion the FA Cup with a last gasp save at Wembley on 21 May 1983.

United celebrate their FA Cup Final replay victory against Brighton and Hove Albion in time-honoured fashion at Wembley on 26 May 1983.

Bryan Robson beats Liverpool's Alan Kennedy to the loose ball to score for United during the Charity Shield clash at Wembley on 20 August 1983.

Bryan Robson with Barcelona captain, Diego Maradona, ahead of the European Cup Winners' Cup quarter-final second leg at Old Trafford on 21 March 1984.

Graeme Hogg battles with David Preece of Luton Town at Kenilworth Road on 21 April 1985.

United's Kevin Moran (fourth right) becomes the first player to be sent off in an FA Cup Final at Wembley on 18 May 1985.

Peter Davenport duels with Nicky Reid of Manchester City during a League Division One match at Old Trafford on 22 March 1986.

Chris Turner keeping goal for United v Nottingham Forest on 4 October 1986.

Terry Gibson of United challenges Arsenal's Kenny Sansom while Tony Adams looks on: Old Trafford, 24 January 1987.

Brian Laws of Nottingham Forest takes to the air to deny United's Ralph Milne during an FA Cup quarter final encounter: Old Trafford, 18 March 1989.

Mike Duxbury in action during a League Division One match at Millwall on 10 February 1990.

Alex Ferguson in his office at Old Trafford shortly after his appointment in November 1986.

United photocall 1987: Graeme Hogg, Paul McGrath, Viv Anderson, Chris Turner and Norman Whiteside look on.

Portrait of John Sivebaek, circa 1987.

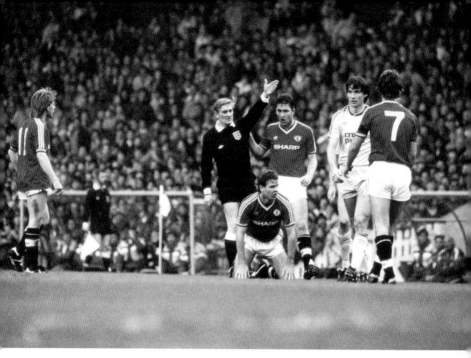

Goalscorer Norman Whiteside speaks to the ref during United's 1-1 draw with Liverpool at Old Trafford on 15 November 1987.

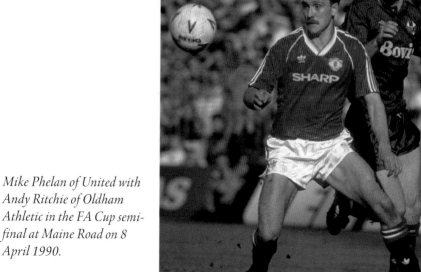

Mike Phelan of United with Andy Ritchie of Oldham Athletic in the FA Cup semi-final at Maine Road on 8 April 1990.

In the early days he was the manager who gave me the strongest platform for my ability with the standard of the team he built at Aberdeen and his discipline and organisation.

His confrontational methods helped me to develop my mental strength. If I could handle Fergie, then as a player or manager I felt I could handle almost anything.

However, I would only single him out as having had the greatest influence on me in relation to one aspect of my career.

As for the other parts, notably when I was more experienced and thus more receptive to a less controlling and dictatorial form of management, I owe just as much (if not more) to men such as Ron Atkinson and Howard Wilkinson.

As much as I admire Fergie for what he has achieved, I have to admit that this is offset by the memories of the deterioration in our relationship.

As indicated by his comments about our time together in his 1999 autobiography *Managing My Life*, it would seem that Fergie is not too enamoured with me either.

Those comments which related mainly to my desire to leave Aberdeen and Manchester United, and included Fergie saying I 'could not be trusted an inch' surprised and disappointed me.

I know I made one or two mistakes in my dealings with him but I feel there were mitigating circumstances. One of the problems in my relationship with him was that the longer we worked together, the more I needed him to adopt a different attitude and approach with me.

I needed him to treat me as an adult, not a kid – to have some respect for the fact that I was an experienced professional to whom abuse from the manager had become more of a motivational turn-off than a stimulus.

Not long after he joined me at Manchester United and took up from where he had left off with me at Aberdeen, I remember telling him, 'Listen, you spoke to me like that nine years ago. It might have worked then but it is not going to work now.' But the screaming and shouting did not cease – it just got worse and more personal.

His behaviour made me think that he looked on my decision to leave Aberdeen as a personal slight. At team meetings he would say, 'Where do you think you're going? Who would want a crap player like you?'

In November 1986 he joined me at Old Trafford. It was a great move for him and Manchester United but not, as it turned out, a great move for me.

I had loved playing for Atkinson at United. After being beaten with a big stick for so long at Aberdeen, it was refreshing to have a manager who trusted me and appreciated me and treated me like an adult.

Mal Donaghy was brought in: a 31-year-old utility defender from Luton Town. Sell a creative midfielder when we are desperate for goals and bring in a journeyman defender. This frankly bizarre juxtaposition seemed to sum up where we were: coherent transfer policy is always the first casualty of a manager under pressure. I was with Flynny on United Road at the Derby County game on 15 April 1989. The tannoy announced the semi-final at Hillsborough between Forest and Liverpool had been stopped just a few minutes in. Information was sketchy but various blokes with radios said something really bad had happened. Just before the end of the match the tannoy further announced that there were believed to be fatalities. I can remember the haunting quietness of the crowd in those last few minutes. As we left the ground and got the train, more news filtered through. We realised how lucky we were to be going home at all.

Friday, 26 May 1989. I played cricket at Toft early that balmy, late-spring evening. I was out for an elegant 0 bowled around my legs: I am sure their umpire gave me the wrong guard. Truth be told I couldn't concentrate knowing Arsenal needed to beat Liverpool at Anfield by two clear goals to win the title and I would be missing the first half at least. I arrived back to see Alan Smith put the Gunners ahead just after the break. With Arsenal still 1-0 up Steve McMahon gestured there was one minute left and to put the ball in the corner. That was that: they had not even won the title on goal difference, but goals scored. A minute or so later, why on earth didn't John Barnes heed McMahon's sage advice? Head to the corner flag at the Kop End and hoof the ball to Widnes instead of turning inside and being robbed by Kevin Richardson? It was an expensive piece of total football. Lukic to Dixon to Smith to Thomas. You know the rest. Of course, it was perfectly acceptable for Arsenal to win the title on goals scored.

At the time that was one of the best days of my life. And I wasn't alone. United fans on our street went crazy. It felt better than both our FA Cup wins put together. But why? When does competition become an obsession? What drives a United fan to have Ramos 18 on the back of his/her shirt after the Salah incident in the Champions League Final? People say it's historic and economic, but no one cares about cotton or canals anymore. It's simpler than that, I think. When you are happy and content in yourself do you care about what is happening on the other side of the fence? Not really. You might take a peek from time to time, but you don't springboard over it in black clothes in the dead of night to pull up a tree and place creosote in its roots. If we'd have had a European Cup Final to look forward to in 1989 would we have been so emotionally invested in events on Merseyside that night? Course not. When you are finishing 11th what else do you have? It's about hope and displacement; it's far better to hate them than begin to hate ourselves because that in itself is unthinkable. I am sure many Liverpool fans will remember the Aguero moment in a similar context. At least mobile phones were not commonplace in 1989. They could hide under the duvet for a week. We could not avoid it.

Act 9

Awaiting On You All

No one likes the end of an era, or the end of anything for that matter. We can get used to the good, the bad and the downright ugly in this life and accept it for what it is but changing horses is always more difficult. It was sad to see Whiteside and McGrath leave. Neil Webb and Mike Phelan came in. Webb was an elegant midfield player with a superb range of passing and had already formed a promising partnership at England level with Bryan Robson. Phelan was not an elegant midfield player. Nor did he have a superb range of passing. Nor had he played for England. A crumbling stadium infrastructure is replaced by a better one. The playing infrastructure is no different. You can't contemplate Gazza one summer and sign Mike Phelan the next. That was prima facie evidence that we were going nowhere fast. And we were paying over the odds for mediocrity too. Mal Donaghy cost £650,000 from Luton Town; Phelan cost £750,000 from Norwich City; Strachan was sold to Leeds United for £300,000. You might take a punt on a young lad from Luton or Norwich but paying big money for players from these outfits in their late 20s and early 30s? None of it made sense. If Webb was playing alongside Robson what was Phelan's role? Right-midfield? Full-back? Attacking midfield? His goalscoring record of nine in 156 for Norwich and nine in 168 for Burnley before that was the strike rate of Frank Spencer, not Frank Lampard. Whenever I saw him in later years as Ferguson's assistant on the bench with his shorts on, I entered into some form of Kafkaesque shock: the frosted sweat of bad memories told me he was about to come on.

There was little cause for optimism when the reigning champions Arsenal arrived at a sun-drenched Old Trafford on the opening day of the 1989/90 season. But we need not have feared. Is it a bird? Is it a plane? No. But there was definitely something emerging from the silhouette shadow of the Kellogg's factory on Trafford Park. It was Superman himself: Michael Knighton. On the eve of the Arsenal game, this former PE teacher and Coventry City trialist from Derbyshire had apparently agreed to buy Martin Edward's controlling share for £10 million (with a similar amount offered to the other shareholders) through a specific-purpose, Isle of Man-based company bankrolled by a number of high-profile investors including Bob Thornton and Stanley Cohen. He also vowed to plough £10 million of funds into the redevelopment of Old Trafford and use the inelastic demand and emotional attachment of the supporters to maximise brand marketing, merchandising and television revenues. Contracts were apparently signed.

In a *Daily Telegraph* article dated 17 August 2009, Neil Webb takes up the story:

We had heard about the takeover, but this chap came into the dressing room before the game, introduced himself as the new owner and then asked for a kit!

We thought he just wanted to join in with the warm-up, but I couldn't believe what I was seeing when he ran on to the pitch and whacked the ball into the net at the Stretford End.

It was hilarious, really. Unbelievable. He just decided that he wanted to go out there and have his own little cameo role.

It was the kind of thing that football chairmen just don't do and we all wondered what was going on, but it turned out that Knighton didn't have the money. Martin Edwards pulled out of the deal.

You just wouldn't read about it. Well, you are reading about it but even by United's lackadaisical standards of the day this is incredibly bad. Why did no one check he had the money? Or check that his backers did? Was there no due diligence done at all? No audit? No security review? No valuation? No loan notes? Did Martin Edwards not ask him to provide a bank statement or at least a few heavy-looking NatWest porcelain pigs as collateral? Surely United had a phalanx of lawyers, advisers and forensic accountants checking all this out? Bryan Robson may be to blame a bit as well. When Knighton asked for a kit in the dressing room he could have said 'fuck off' and show us the money, or 'I'm the England captain, who the fuck are you?' In a *GQ* magazine interview with Andy Mitten dated 1 September 2017 Edwards explains the background: 'The

Knighton thing didn't do me any good,' Edwards concedes of the infamous proposed takeover in 1989. 'I was in debt to the bank, I was under pressure and smoking heavily. I knew the Stretford End needed to be rebuilt. And things were not going well on the pitch. I was getting a lot of abuse, even at games, where people would shout at the directors' box.

'I didn't actually see Knighton's shenanigans – I was still in the directors' room entertaining visiting guests – but I caught it later on the news,' he admits. 'It's become an iconic moment, but at the time I was fuming. The deal hadn't been finalised yet. He was jumping the gun. That was really the first sign that something wasn't quite right about Knighton – it was reckless and his decision-making really worried me; others felt the same way. The fans loved it, but it was one of the worst possible moves he could have made. Even Knighton himself, in hindsight, has admitted it was a mistake. Why did he do it? Who knows? Maybe for publicity purposes. Whatever the reason, it raised huge questions in my mind, such that I now had severe doubts.'

So, he wasn't checked out properly because Edwards was smoking and needed the money? It just gets better. Perhaps Knighton missed a trick? Maybe 20 Regal King Size would have done the job? With a few Focus Points he could have claimed a solar-panelled calculator as a free gift to work out that the mathematics did not make any sense. Normally bad deals are condemned as 'back of a fag packet' but that's all this one needed. It's the same analogy I used above about the law firm who gets a half-plausible client half on board and thinks it will be jam tomorrow and

burgers and beers with Whoopi Goldberg by Whitsun.
Deep down we know the truth: hubris, arrogance and
greed prevent us from grasping it. And, I guess, the fear
of the alternative. But this wasn't some tinpot law firm,
this was Manchester United; he owed duties to each
and every one of us, not just himself and his boardroom
cronies. Could you imagine the same Fred Karno's circus
passing for half-normal at Arsenal or Liverpool or Celtic
or Rangers? Edwards was a decent man under pressure,
but really? Surely there was some infrastructure around
him? Someone to say no.

Knighton set out his own thoughts in a *Guardian*
interview with Paul Mitten dated 27 November 2019:

> I think history has proved without question that
> in 1989 I knew what the future held for the whole
> industry, not just Manchester United. Everyone
> I talked to back then was sceptical about satellite
> television but I knew it would be a gamechanger.
> I could see that football, and particularly English
> football, would soon be worth billions as a global
> product.
>
> It seemed obvious to me to get hold of one
> of the greatest brands in the sector would be like
> owning a gold mine, but at the time I was pretty
> much alone in that view. The *Financial Times*
> asked me why I was buying a club that had just
> announced a loss of £1.3m and was only turning
> over £7m a year. I said I was buying potential, that
> I thought it should be possible to turn United into
> the world's wealthiest club.

He was bang on there! United floated on the stock exchange in 1993 with a valuation of £47 million and was acquired by the Glazers in 2005 for £790m. According to *Forbes* United were worth £3 billion as at May 2019. How Knighton must have wished he could find that extra money and how Edwards must be glad he kept his shares! When his backers pulled out Knighton did receive some shares and a seat on the board so let's not feel too sorry for him. He also now spends his time creating artworks and poetry – alright for some.

You do not care too much about the internecine workings of the boardroom when you are 14. I was getting more and more into The Stone Roses anyway: even now I'd take art over politics any day of the week and twice on a Sunday. Flynny's stepdad bought the first album in 1989 on vinyl and we played it to death during the summer of 1989. It would become a new religion. Even now I can name each song on that record in order, just as readily as any cup-winning United team. We used the Rusholme Sunday markets to get the psychedelic baggy jerseys and Joe Bloggs jeans and starched our fishing hats into oblivion to get the Reni vibe going on. Knowing they were United fans helped a lot too: if they were City or worse it might have been tricky. How would that have gone? You can't be Christian during the week and then Hindu or Muslim at the weekend no more than you can ride two bikes with one arse. Maybe Dad had founded religion or turned to the Hacienda himself? Just before the Arsenal game he decided to give me pocket money: a fiver a week as long as I mowed the lawn and picked up the clippings. He was also happy for me to resume a paper round and go to

United games with my mates. He even allowed me to stop the tennis lessons. Something was not right. He wanted us to be 'friends', whatever that meant.

Flynny was a lad of deep superstition and an eternal optimist. So, our travails the previous season were not in his view down to Ferguson or Ralph Milne or Mal Donaghy, but United Road. It was an odd part of the ground. They would sing 'The Stretford End is full of shit' which made no sense to me at all. I had yet to read *Animal Farm*. Flynny was confident that returning to the Stretford End would restore our fortunes. As Knighton smashed the ball in the Stretford End, I remember no one really gave a shit. You got that kind of stuff quite a lot back then. There was the odd 'you robbing bastard' but most of us assumed he had done a parachute jump for charity or was about to climb Everest in fingerless gloves for Manchester's homeless. I can remember more clearly that day a meat pie with sauce flying through the stratosphere and landing on some poor bastard's head. As he turned around to ask 'who the fuck did that?' about 10,000 fingers gave him the answer.

You know what they say about after the Lord Mayor's Show? After a double hundred partnership the new batsman gets a first-baller. So, following the Michaels and meat pies of the day it was almost inevitable that a fine Arsenal side would give us a doing over. But the tinsel and trumpets continued. We won 4-1. Neil Webb scored an absolute cracker at the Stretford End. Webb was not only a brilliant passer of the ball, but he had a goal in him: prior to joining United he had already scored over 100 league goals which was pretty impressive. He looked the finished article but just a couple of weeks later he shattered his Achilles tendon playing for England and that was that. A real shame. Mike Phelan came into the side on a more regular basis. Later that autumn we bought big: Gary Pallister for £2.3 million from Middlesbrough (a British record fee for a defender and the second-highest fee to be paid by a British club), Paul Ince for £1.8 million from West Ham, and Danny Wallace for £1.2 million from Southampton. These were huge gambles by Ferguson for unproven players. There was more than an element of last throw of the dice. At least they were all young and talented, and not Mal Donaghy, Ralph Milne or Mike Phelan.

I've said nothing about Man City, have I? Why would I? They were far worse than us in the 1980s, ergo, completely irrelevant. There were no noisy neighbours back then and if people in blue sang about Lee, Bell and Summerbee they'd be laughed at or locked up; now it's all royal blood and New York feeder clubs they are the greatest triumvirate of footballers Britain has ever produced. Maybe as part of the nascent friends thing Dad decided that we would go to Maine Road together on 23 September 1989 to watch City take on United. There was some banter on the M56 that early afternoon. 'Who was the last team in Manchester to win the First Division, Jamie?' No one likes being on the wrong end of a binary question. A year after our last triumph in 1967 City claimed the title with a 4-3 win at Newcastle on the last day. Dad was there of course, along with the three million others who were not. Maybe he was at Shea Stadium in 1965 as well? Maybe he introduced The Beatles to Ed Sullivan? World Cup Final? He was next to the Queen: all snot and marmite.

'Why wasn't it like this more often?' I thought. Why was he generally angry? Why had it taken him more than 14 years to tell me that he went to the 1968 United v Benfica European Cup Final? And that he was the only person out of 100,000 at Wembley wanting Eusébio's men to win the gargantuan trophy? I know now of course: life is a shin pad of stress, not a load of free shiny-badge Panini stickers. But keep the shin pad to yourself: that's your job. The stickers belonged to me.

I recall some pretty horrendous scenes on the way to the ground amongst rival factions: stomach-churning scenes which made my red colours shrink deep into me like a painful hernia. Dad's fault again. Park nearer the ground and pay a fiver. He would risk life and limb to save 50p and just out of love he would risk mine as well.

Thanks Dad. Somewhere near Wilmslow Road but miles away from the stadium some young lad asked, 'Quid to mind your car, mate?' As red battered blue and blue battered red we somehow arrived at the ground in one piece. I was surprised to see how dilapidated and disparate Maine Road was compared with our cantilever model: a real Victorian shit heap. Of course, Dad bought tickets in the worst part of the ground (six quid for him and three for me) which meant that I could see more of the giant pillar with advanced concrete cancer than anything else. He then gleefully turned around, told me this was my treat and there'd be no pocket money this week, nor in fact until April because the grass would not need cutting until then. At least I had my paper round. I kind of knew instinctively that I was in more trouble than Carl Bridgewater at Yew

Tree Farm in that horrible pen by the corner flag nearest to the Scoreboard End. I just hoped the concrete pillar would last 90 minutes before succumbing to the inevitable; even if it did the army of United fans who had inveigled their way into the cheap seats (cheers again, Dad) would probably deep-fry us before half-time. They ran riot for the first half hour of the game at least.

And you know when it's really kicking off and people carry on regardless? Many years later I got caught out in a London pub: the densely packed mass of badly beaten northern bodies was far higher than the bar itself but the locals casually found a loose brick of life and light: 'Pint of Pride please, Gloria' as if nothing had happened. It was the same here. As patent leather thudded into cranium the City anthem gaily rang out: 'City, Manchester City, We are the lads who are made to win' and Helen the Bell at the front of the Scoreboard End merrily rang away as if demanding orange pekoe and scones on a rectangular silver tray.

Dad was hard and not frightened. I was not hard and frightened. I buried my frightened face deep into the rag of the programme which I had just paid for out of my pocket money. At least Robson was playing. Maybe we could get him in here and sort this mess out. Or get him on the megaphone to restore order. His presence in any capacity made things seem a bit safer. The stadium announcer had other ideas: rather than just do his job he excitedly added that the United skipper had cried off with a shin injury picked up in the midweek League Cup game against Portsmouth.

Here is how we lined up that afternoon:

1. Jim Leighton
2. Viv Anderson
3. Mal Donaghy
4. Mike Duxbury
5. Mike Phelan
6. Gary Pallister
7. Russell Beardsmore
8. Paul Ince
9. Brian McClair
10. Mark Hughes
11. Danny Wallace.

City attacked the Scoreboard End in the first half and raced into a 3-0 lead at the break. Britain's most expensive central defender spent the entire period on his backside, run ragged by the twin strike force of Ian Oldfield and Trevor Morley. Dad was cock-a-hoop. 'Pallister is 6ft 4! I didn't know they stacked shit that high?! He should put a pair of boots on his fucking arse!'

Shortly after the interval Hughes spectacularly volleyed home to reduce the arrears: it was a wonderful strike. Fortunately, as it turned out, I could only see one strip of the pitch that day, but this was sufficient for me to see Hughes stop, steady, contort and execute. Worth the entrance fee alone now but not then. As City made it 5-1 after about an hour, I can recall the Platt Lane end of the ground which housed the United fans pretty much emptying. That might have prevented a full-scale riot. Abiding memory? Jeers when Russell Beardsmore was replaced by Lee Sharpe: Beardsmore was our best player that day. That's how bad it had become. Dad was murder for leaving games early to miss the traffic. You know one of those? Watch Eric Clapton play one note of 'Layla' at the Albert Hall, then it's time for the ring road and the bypass. I hated all that. Not that day I didn't. He was unbearable until he discovered the car was minus a window and a car stereo. I pissed myself inside: a well-deserved pyrrhic victory on a day I almost did not see out. I just hoped it was a United fan!

Ferguson, in a Cynthia Bateman article reprinted by *The Guardian* on 23 September 2009, opined that this was the worst defending he had seen in his managerial career: 'It was like climbing a glass mountain,' he said. In that case, why play Mike Duxbury and Mal Donaghy in the back four? Hardly Edmund Hillary, were they?

Years did not mellow Ferguson's bitter memories of that day, as he recalled in his autobiography, *Managing My Life*: 'We were slaughtered 5-1 in the most embarrassing defeat of my management career. After the game, I went straight home, got into bed, and put the pillow over my head. A sense of guilt had engulfed me.'

In the same *Guardian* article Gary Pallister describes the loss as 'some form of nadir'. He takes up the story and the radioactive fallout:

> [Steve Bruce and Bryan Robson were out injured but] there was no excuse. The funny thing was that we started off really well, playing lovely football, but then there was trouble behind one of the goals which spilled over to the side of the pitch, and the players were taken off. After that, everything City

hit went in. I'd say it was the lowest point of my entire career.

Pallister described Ferguson as 'in shock after the game, practically speechless' and remembers returning to training on Monday at the Cliff after spending the weekend in Middlesbrough with his family:

> There was no security and when I walked from the dressing room there were four burly United fans waiting for me outside the door. They told me I wasn't fit to wear a United shirt, we shouldn't have sold Paul McGrath, I was a 'disgrace' to the club, the whole treatment. I thought it was just me, but it turned out that all the lads had got abuse from these guys. They really ripped into us and it was quite frightening.

Lots of one-sided hyperbole but can a silver lining ever be found? Andy Hinchcliffe, who scored City's fifth that day, argued persuasively, in a BBC Sport article by Phil McNulty dated 4 November 2011, that this defeat shaped the thinking behind the modern Manchester United:

> We were looking at what we thought was a watershed moment for City and it probably turned into a watershed moment for United in the way they approached things after that game.
>
> After we beat them at Maine Road, Sir Alex realised that things needed to change, things needed to be done very differently because that

was unacceptable from his point of view. I think it made Sir Alex realise that sometimes you bring all these players in but it's not going to be sudden transformation. City and other clubs have discovered that, when you spend a lot of money and bring top players in, it's not always easy to gel them into a side and make it work. That game underlined that. City had four or five youngsters in the side and we turned them over 5-1. Maybe it made Sir Alex and the players realise that, if United were to be successful, things needed to be done differently? They learned very quickly from their mistakes.

I think a defeat on that scale against their local rivals accelerated a change of emphasis in the way Sir Alex did things.

He learned lessons in terms of some of the youngsters that he brought in later on. He looked at City and the way they were producing young players. I was part of a youth system that produced five or six players for the first team – and I think that changed Fergie's thinking about how he approached things at United. Young players were brought in through the system and made a fantastic contribution.

It's a fair point by one of football's more intelligent pundits. Lee Sharpe did well that season; so too did Lee Martin; Mark Robins was introduced as well. The season after saw Giggs make his bow and Scholes, Beckham, Butt and Neville would, of course, follow. But Ferguson had always believed in youth anyway: he brought through Alex

McLeish, Jim Leighton, Mark McGhee, John Hewitt and
Eric Black amongst others at Aberdeen. He could hardly
buy his way to success there could he? Youth was probably
always his intention at United. But a 14-year-old Beckham
was not going to help him this season, not unless he could
magic some balm from his Russell Spinner Coca-Cola
yo-yo to fix the broken bones of his England midfielders.
When he put the pillow over his head that evening, he
must have realised he either needed to press hard or have
a bit of good old-fashioned luck in the FA Cup. Or check
the train times to Aberdeen.

Act 10

Behind That Locked Door

No moping in Super Ted pyjamas for Flynny and I: we were more passionate than ever. We even went to the reserve games now: they were free if you were a member. So, when our first team were losing against Charlton Athletic at Selhurst Park in early November 1989 we went to Old Trafford to see our second string take on Liverpool. On arrival at the ground we literally bumped into Mike Duxbury locking down his 1988 BMW 325i: 'You're a wanker, Duxbury!' 'You're shit, Duxbury!' 'Duxbury, you're a dickhead!'

What's odd about that? Liverpool fans abusing United players. Nothing, save that no Liverpool fans were present. It was a reserve game. Of course, it was our own fans. Flynny now had the confidence of Ian Brown and, he thought, the United minerals of Sir Matt himself. 'You're fucking wank, Duxbury!'

I did not join in the chorus. I probably should have been more outraged, but it was kind of funny and my mind was elsewhere. I remember thinking if a terrible player gets wheels like this what will I get when I have my A level and degree? A private jet? A sedan chair to the match? A cruise missile? That's what they tell you, isn't it? The Mr Greens and Mrs Todds of this world. What do you get? A bus ticket and a bedsit? I kept my side of the bargain and I had the pieces of paper to prove it. No wonder I used to be so bloody angry.

Between 1985 and 1990 and before the Taylor Report which was the death knell for standing at top-flight grounds, there were two layers to each of the four sides of Old Trafford: each side had terracing at the lower level and seats at the top in stands conveniently labelled A–L. The Stretford End standing terrace was nowhere near as big as you might think, not like the vast Kop or North Bank at Highbury. Stand E cast a huge shadow over Groundside Stretford, as it was officially called: it went a third or so down that famous side of the ground but good luck seeing anything in those seats! Moving clockwise left from the Stretford End we then had Stand F in the corner (always good for a spare seat or two for a shitty game) and Stands G, H, I which were for season-ticket holders and overlooked the United Road terracing. Stand J was a bit of a graveyard in the corner and often kept clear for segregation purposes. Then behind the other goal we had Stand K which overlooked the away supporters in the terrace below. In the far corner we had Stand L which was the family stand sponsored by Panini stickers where I watched the West Ham game back in August 1985. Moving round further we had the good seats of Stands A–D (C had the best mid-pitch view) and the Stretford Paddock below.

It was odd to see the ground so empty for the reserve game, but I looked forward to seeing all these youngsters we kept hearing about in despatches. Andy Rammell? David Wilson? Derek Brazil? Brian Carey? Wayne Bullimore? Paul McGuinness? Wayne Heseltine? No, nor me. No wonder Ferguson was drawing the curtains before *'Allo 'Allo!* and *Casualty*. No Ryan Giggs: maybe he was with the first team? For the experience? That old classic: the experience of learning to lose at Charlton. I remember us losing 2-1: Mark Bosnich was in goal (although I had to look that up) and Viv Anderson was at the back. A 17-year-old Steve McManaman was an unused substitute for Liverpool that day – I wonder if he thought the Stretford End was small as well.

We half expected some grief at this fixture, but we went because we knew there would be none if that makes sense. As a true sign of our bravery we went nowhere near the Chelsea game a few weeks later. But I was fortified a touch by braving Liverpool for the first time and coming back in one piece.

'Dad, can I go to London?' 'London? Bloody London?' It could well be a scene out of *The Royle Family*, or *This is England*. That's why those shows are so good. At some point or other every northerner asks this question: it's a rite of passage just as treacherous as any unplanned pregnancy, shotgun wedding, hangover or tattoo. It's actually much trickier than you think because it's your mum who puts lolly sticks in the spokes; while Dad thinks it's bold and adventurous, Mum is convinced you will meet Jack the Ripper or Dennis Nilsen at Euston Station: that, or take a wrong train and get murdered on the Orient Express.

Dad's noes can become a yes but Mum's noes are more of a 'kind of' no which gives extra wife grief to Dad and ensures that a no stays exactly there. A very firm do-not-ask-again no.

Highbury was planned for the next away trip on Sunday, 3 December 1989. I learnt that once you have dropped the bombshell you need to back it up really quickly with hard facts which cannot be disputed, facts which make you look like a hard-working, well-behaved lad who has been brought up properly and deserves a day out in the cold and rain. A lad who is a credit to you and who you should be proud of. Flattery is fine but don't let them speak at this point. The odd 'Ah, that's nice' is OK but nothing more. Don't turn it into a sob story or a competition. They don't care that David Flynn goes to 18s already and takes ecstasy like smarties. Remember: hard and flattery gets you on the coach. Then they have to say 'OK'. If they don't, do it anyway: you did ask nicely. It probably went a bit like this:

'So, since I've started my GCSEs my grades have improved as you know from parents evening. Mrs Jackson asked whether there is any French in my family as I'm so good at it. Since my paper round in August I've earned £60 and after I have bought your birthday presents and Christmas, I've 35 quid left …'

'Ah that's nice of you, Jamie.'

'Did Mrs Jackson really say that?'

'So, I was wondering if I could go on the coach to the United game at Highbury. It's an organised club coach. All official. It goes straight to the ground and back; they'll be no murders or going underground or anything like that. I'm a bit gutted about not making the inter-league team as well so this might cheer me up a bit.'

'Sure, you can Jamie. You've earned it.'

The inter-league bit was true. How Bob Holland from Eagle was a better centre-forward than me defied football common sense. It was a bit like picking Francis Jeffers over Teddy Sheringham. Were the coaches not watching the games? Did they not look at the table (we were top, and Eagle were nowhere) or the goalscoring charts? (I was top, and Bob Holland was nowhere.) Alex Ferguson, Terry Venables, Glenn Hoddle, Kevin Keegan and Sven-Göran Eriksson would be selecting Phil Neville next. Back then when you were angry you wrote letters: it was a bit easier as 14-year-olds could write more than a sentence without moaning and/or their hand falling off and you could buy seven second-class stamps for a quid and still have enough change for a 10p mix bag. So, I wrote to Phil Neal at Bolton Wanderers setting out my goalscoring record and asked for a trial: maybe I scored too many for his liking as I never heard back. Anyway, while Bob Holland was (hopefully) getting both legs broken and/or serious ligament damage somewhere in Whiston I would be on the coach with the boys – I wasn't complaining.

Flynny knew a face or two now; he also had an embryonic beard to accompany The Stone Roses clobber. It meant that he could get served at Kinnery's, the local grocery in Stockton Heath. He had about 24 cans of

Special Brew, 36 Strongbow ciders and 60 Embassy Number 1s. As the coach left Goodies in town at about 9am that morning to head south he got stuck in. The chimes of 'Waterfall' confirmed this was a Sunday with a difference. As we got to somewhere near Stafford, I got every lyric to '(Song For My) Sugar Spun Sister' bang on. Daz Morgan, who was one of the hard lads from Bewsey, was impressed: there were no lyric sheets and internet in those days so you needed *Top of the Pops* recording skills to know when to stop and start the shagged-out tape and the trained ear of repeated practice.

'Every what?' he asked. 'Every Member of Parliament trips on glue, Daz.' 'How can you make out they're saying that?' 'Practice, Daz.' 'Do you think they do?' 'Do what?' 'Members of Parliament trip on glue?' 'Yeah, probably.' 'Do you think "Elizabeth My Dear" is about Elizabeth McIntrye at your school?' 'Could be.' 'I'll put a word in for you if you want?' 'Will ya?' 'Sure.'

And with that I was in. It wasn't Rashford, Pogba and Fred: it was lager, cider and bed. I was ruined by Northampton and crashed out. Fittingly just before London I woke up to 'I Am The Resurrection' and a sore head which didn't need Reni's drum intro. 'Get a whisky in!' implored Daz. It was nice to get that physical dependence side of things in the locker straight away. I then heard 'Where Is My Mind' by the Pixies for the first time. It was a pretty apposite question to ask as mine was somewhere between a shed and a sling. Do you ever wish you could hear things again for the first time? Joey Santiago's riff and solo on that track would be near the top of my list. Then there was the classic 'Are we in London yet?' Northerners will refuse to believe it until the Thames floods the motorway carrying Big Ben, Buck House and Prince Philip as detritus. As the whisky and coke kicked in, The Charlatans took over the sound waves; the lack of football songs was an enduring memory of that day. Football culture was changing for me: it was more about the clothes and the fun and the tunes and the party. This was our Blackpool Charabanc of the 40s and 50s: as long as we had The Ink Spots and the accordion and the bottles of stout it didn't matter if it was shit when we got there.

We were expecting a bit of trouble when we got off the coach. That's what happens in London, isn't it? Thank God we had Daz Morgan's penknife to keep the Red Army at bay: we could have been in the French Foreign Legion the next day manicuring lawns with finger scissors. But there was nothing apart from the odd 'You Northern Slags' as the police took us into the Drayton Park pub which housed away fans. Daz Morgan's advice was always to order something out of the ordinary if you want to get served. He thought it made you look more seasoned. 'Two snakebites and black with blue curaçao and four spiced rums please.' 'Fuck off you ponce!'

Other than the apocryphal stories about deep dark London, I'm not sure why we expected a battle royale. This was a cold December Sunday afternoon in Highbury and Islington; the game was live on ITV. Attendance: 34,484: they were all in their bijou three-storey Victorian houses watching Brian Walden cremate Thatcher over roast beef and Yorkshire puddings and proper red wine. Who could blame them? This is where I now live. When I see away fans stumbling towards the Emirates, I always remember my first excursion. It's like a full circle thing: when I wake up one morning thinking my mum is making packet soup with a whisk, I'll know my time is up.

It was freezing cold on the exposed, open terraces at the corner of the Clock End side of the ground. I can remember it was a shit game and we played in blue and we lost. If I had the energy to blame the blue shirts I would have done. How the hell is it feasibly possible for United to play in blue? Whose ridiculous brainchild was that? It's just plain wrong. Can you enjoy *Laurel and Hardy* in colour? Have City ever played in red? Have Liverpool ever played in blue? Exactly. I defy anyone to name one important game we won in blue: it will by now not surprise you that I can name plenty we have lost. I also remember the singing lacked the variety and imagination of Goodison Park the year before: save the odd desultory 'Hughesy, Hughesy' or 'There's only one Bryan Robson' there was not much else. Maybe everyone had legged it for the first lap or two of the 10,000 metres and was now regretting it, cold and pissed off regretting it. I learnt an important lesson: don't be hungover at games, Jamie. Either be stone-cold sober or rat-arsed pissed in the future.

On the way back was a different matter. We tore into the remaining bevvy and I learnt another important lesson: never underestimate the strength of the second wind.

> We are just one of those teams
> That you see now and then
> We often score six
> But we seldom score ten
> We beat 'em at home

And we beat 'em away
We kill any bastards
That get in our way
We are the pride of all Europe
The cock of the North
We hate the Scousers
The Cockneys of course
We are United
Without any doubt
We are the Manchester boys, nah, nah, nah …

It was nearly Christmas as well:

Bryan Robson's our messiah …
He's got the devils breathing fire
He taught us to play
The United Way
And guide us to a Wembley wonderland
Jingle bells
Jingle bells
Jingle all the way
Oh what fun it is to see
United win away.

It was definitely not 'Mistletoe and Wine' when I got home. I never know why people bollock you when you are that pissed? Do they not know you are not listening and it's actually making the day a bit better and a whole lot funnier? Wait until the morning, but they never do: by then it's all buckets and bananas and dried toast. School was not good: it was that bad that Flynny and I had to wait until the Tuesday to laugh about the fun and games. Yes, that bad! I ran out of Science to be spectacularly sick into someone's locker and I spent the PSE class lying face down in the toilet cubicle doorway praying for peace or capital punishment. So what if Norman Bates had just pissed his Sugar Puffs all over it? I just didn't care. Weil's disease or any form of chronic leptospirosis seemed a good option around 11am on Monday, 4 December 1989. I also had to play football that afternoon in a five-a-side tournament. I didn't leave the centre circle until Mr Allen dragged me off. 'No wonder you're not in the inter-league side, Magill.' Fuck off, Allen. Even Mr Riley chimed in and he didn't even teach me anymore! 'People who pick Business Studies and Manchester United get the airy-fairy jobs, Magill. People who pick History and Liverpool get the good jobs.'

How the hell did he know what I had been up to? Did he see me dying on the TV? Those orange luminous gloves had breathed their last; the New York Giants cap (all the way from America I was told) hadn't helped much either. Or had Flynny perked up a bit in front of Laura Kent? Fit granted. But no chance. Not even for him. Was a no ever worth it? Surely not when he knew her active media juggernaut, which picked up every blob of weekend sick and chip paper, would lead all the way to Mr Tasker's office by afternoon break. Riley had not forgiven me for not selecting History for GCSE. The guaranteed 'A' grade might have given him a whisky bonus. Not that he needed it: he reeked of the stuff permanently. A horrible drunk is a horrible drunk whether it is sprinkled with icing sugar and has letters after its name, or not; he talked the bollocks of irrelevant battles as well: Matthew Leigh picked History and Liverpool and he ended up working as a pet-food taster and married a self-certified fraudster with delusional tendencies. By evening I was fine, and I think Dad was quietly impressed at my performance: I guess it is one of those proud moments in the life and times of a father. Killer hangover 1 in the kit bag.

What's a nadir? According to *Oxford Advanced Learner's Dictionary*: 'the worst moment of a particular situation'. For Ferguson this arrived when we lost at home to Crystal Palace on 9 December 1989. My hangover had just about cleared, and I knew with the London incident not far enough behind me that I was very lucky to be within a million miles of the game. Dad's mate had bought tickets for me and his son ages before so it would have been unfair to call it off on the account of one piss artist. I was warned in advance to stick to Shandy Bass and not to mix my drinks.

This was the first time ever I had the best seats: the C stand quite high up by the halfway line. I remember they cost £6.60. We arrived at the ground about 1pm for some reason and I had never met this lad before. He was called Michael; he liked Lisa Stansfield and he was a Liverpool fan. This was going to be a long afternoon. Maybe it was because I was bored shitless, but I do remember the atmosphere. Have you ever worked in a place that you know is about to go under? It's silent; no one is getting bollocked or chased for work; most people are on holiday or off sick if they have not mysteriously disappeared overnight already; unknown blokes with clipboards and beards are strolling around like emperors in waiting. There's a palpable sense that something is about to happen but that might actually be a good thing. Because anything is better than this sterility. No? Well, enjoy your final salary pension – it was like that anyway.

Russell Beardsmore's early opener was hardly celebrated with foaming mouths. All I heard was 'Sparky, give us a wave, Sparky, Sparky, give us a wave.' Ferguson needed goodwill more than most at this time. Goodwill is an easy concept and it's free: it should be your friend; it should mean you overachieve; but most people don't get it at all. You do not piss off your best lawyer by telling him to get back to work at 4.30 on a Friday when he's been on a corporate jolly: you need him more than he needs you; he will leave and you are then left with Ralph Milne. When he fucks it all up it's you who is sacked and struck off. Likewise, you do not piss off your supporters when you need them most for no good reason. In an act of monumental boneheaded idiocy, Ferguson dropped Mark Hughes (a real favourite) and stuck Lee Sharpe up front. Of course, when we went behind, he brings off Sharpe and introduces Hughes far too late. There were mumblings that he wanted to see if McClair could play further up the park without Hughes? Total bollocks if you ask me but if that was the case why not see if Hughes can play without McClair? Bring McClair off. That would at least make some kind of sense. It was the fuzzy thinking of a strangled mind.

I do remember that day seeing the fabled banner: '3 YEARS OF EXCUSES AND IT'S STILL CRAP … TA RA FERGIE.' Peter Molyneux, the chap who unfurled the banner, articulated his feelings some years later in an *Observer* article by Daniel Taylor dated 5 November 2011:

It was a build-up of all the frustrations because his first three years were dark times. Liverpool were running away with everything and we didn't seem to be getting any closer. We were coming off the back of the failures of Dave Sexton and Ron Atkinson to win the league and I just felt the fans had to do something because the club was accepting secondbest.

I was shaking. I loved the club and I was apprehensive people would turn on me but the reaction was amazing. It was like a domino effect around the ground as people realised what the banner said, culminating in this crescendo of cheers and applause.

He was right. We all thought the same. Every single one of us. I do recall the Stretford End singing 'Bryan Robson's Red and White Army'. Great player, great song. I did not appreciate any seditious undertones. Had I done so I would have sung it more heartily. Robson for Ferguson seemed to make perfect sense. We lost again at home the following week to Tottenham and were smashed 3-0 at Villa Park on Boxing Day; 15th in the table.

So why did the axe not fall at Christmas? Howard Kendall must have been considered very seriously this time round. He was available for a start: he had been sacked by Athletic Bilbao in November 1989 and returned home no doubt sick to death of sunshine and paella. Why not give him a call? Invite him round for Mrs Edwards's steak and kidney pie? He went to City a few weeks later but where would he have preferred to go? Maybe City was a short-term thing for him, and he had an eye on the England job which would be available after the 1990 World Cup. United for sure was a long-term project. Jesus: exactly how close did we get to a midfield of Raymond Atteveld, Mike Milligan, John Ebbrell and Gary Ablett circa 1991? George Graham? Interesting but would he have swapped the pots of Highbury for the pans of Old Trafford?

Terry Venables was more viable. He had now exchanged the tapas of Catalonia for the whitebait of White Hart Lane, but he was always on the peripatetic side: a new challenge at a behemoth club like United might have appealed. When people say 'he's a great coach' eyes tend to glaze over; you think of failed managers and traffic cones and bibs and umbrellas and Sammy Lee. But not every top-class player can be wrong about Venables. He might have even brought Gascoigne and Lineker with him? Maybe Chris Waddle too? And he was a firm believer in bringing the young players through too. Crystal Palace remember? OK, so the 'Team of the Eighties' may have been hyperbole but the fact remains that the Palace side which gained promotion to the top flight in 1979 was built around the nucleus of the FA Youth Cup-winning teams of 1977 and 1978. Terry Fenwick, Vince Hilaire, Kenny Sansom et al. He was a good option: maybe a bit cockney flash but lest you forget we had just had Michael Knighton kicking into our fucking net.

Howard Wilkinson? This was the man who made grown men (well, footballers at least) weep buckets at the sight of hills. Martial law was too far to the left for this sergeant major disciplinarian: all burpees, whistles and tracksuits. Perpetually in shorts: he didn't need the stiff breeze of a barbecue in April for the old drumsticks to make an appearance. In the 1980s he gave PE teachers across the land hope: if I flog the lad at the back with the limp and the NHS glasses a bit harder then I might become the manager of Leeds United AFC. At the time he was leading the charge of the mighty Leeds United back to the top flight with staccato, pale ale-flowing football based on the midfield brutality of David Batty and Vinnie Jones and the touch and dexterity of big Lee Chapman up top. He had done well at Sheffield Wednesday and now Leeds and this didn't go unnoticed in those days. He was only 46 too so definitely in the right age demographic. It was certainly a possibility. He went on with Leeds to deprive Ferguson of the title in 1992. Now, if Ferguson had failed to land the title the following year, who knows? It might have been Beckham and Giggs dreading running up another hill, not Brian Marwood and Mel Sterland.

What about Graham Taylor? Even people living on Neptune know that he had taken Watford from the Fourth Division to the top flight in five short years. Did you know Elton John was chairman there too? So many things fall off the radar, don't they? His form was current too: that 1989/90 season saw Aston Villa initially set the pace before finishing second to Kenny Dalglish's men; this meant the Holy Grail of European football the following year. Taylor had the gravitas and the minerals, and he was cool and fashionable. I think that United would have moved heaven and earth to get him. But timing is everything. He had been lined up to replace Bobby Robson the following summer. How soon the FA approached him is not known but at the time the England job probably had more appeal than a rebuild at United. Probably just as well. The summer of 1990 may have seen Kent Nielsen and Steve Sims usurp Bruce and Pallister, Tony Cascarino, Ian Olney and Ian Ormondroyd replace Hughes and McClair up front, and Stuart Gray and Gordon Cowans take over from Bryan Robson in the midfield engine room. Could you imagine him signing Cantona? Look at the approach he took with England too. He had a palpable lack of faith in the minor genius of Gascoigne, Beardsley and Waddle, preferring the more utilitarian characteristics of Geoff Thomas, Andy Sinton, Carlton Palmer and Alan Smith. Do you remember what you were doing on 22 November 1963? I wasn't alive but those of you that were will surely remember where you were and what you were doing when Kennedy was shot. For me the seminal date (and millions of others) is 19 February 1992. The occasion? Geoff Thomas's miss against France. As I tried to balance my organic chemistry equation, I laughed well into 1993. How is it feasibly possible for the ball to leave the foot of an international player in North London and end up in Neptune? Answers on a 165-year orbit postcard please.

Joe Royle had done well at Oldham; ex-United players Steve Coppell and Lou Macari had done well too at Palace and Swindon respectively but in sum the external candidates were either unavailable, not interested or lacking experience. It is sometimes better to be lucky than good: a huge stroke of fortune for Ferguson. What also helped him I think was that caretaker managers were simply not in vogue at the time. But there was a precedent case within the ivory towers of Old Trafford itself. Matt Busby took over from Wilf McGuinness in December 1970 for the remainder of the season. So why not get Bobby Charlton in? OK, he had hardly distinguished himself at Preston North End but that did not matter. He would be steadying the ship (imagine how many times that phrase would have been aired in the ensuing interviews) and buying time to help sell United to a top-bracket manager in the summer: a Kendall or a Venables. Not convinced? OK, well maybe you listened to too many of Bobby's half-time summaries during the BBC's World Cup coverage in the 1980s? Some of them lasted more than 45 minutes. What about Bryan Robson then? Not as caretaker necessarily but as player-manager? Liverpool had done the same with Dalglish a few years earlier and he won the double in his first season. Like Dalglish, Robson was a proper club man in the autumn of a distinguished career; he was respected by the players and adored by the supporters: it made perfect sense. Most things that make perfect sense never happen. Thank God. We may have ended up with Paul Wilkinson and John Hendrie up front.

Act 11

Arnold Grove

I used to love the FA Cup draw. Long before the days of skinny jeans and Rod Stewart it was conducted by two crusty old duffers in regimental-style Football Association blazers. They would summon every remaining sinew of strength from their shrapnel-riven bodies to wrench giant numbered cannonballs from a velvet bag that was pure decadent Regency. There were no buttons back then: it was all heavy lifting. A quick gasp of air and they would exclaim: 'Number 23', hoping against hope and gravity that they would live to lift and announce the next one. You got the feeling it was done after a particularly heavy stilton and port lunch and you were almost catching flies yourself before chief executive Graham Kelly would put a name to the number in his shrill, Bee Gees falsetto and frighten you back to life.

By 1990 it was at least done on the TV: in the mid-80s it was announced on the radio on a Monday lunchtime; if you were off school (by luck or design) you would literally huddle around the wireless to wait for Neville Chamberlain to announce World War III or (even worse) that you had drawn Liverpool away in the third round and that was that for another year. You had to try and make it to a radio: there was nothing worse than Howard Kelly telling you the news. There is something I detest to this day about people who do not like football telling me about football with that conceited 'Did you not know? I thought you liked football' air. Plus, it gave Kelly an excuse to bang on about his Commodore 64 and the Pot Noodle he had snaffled when we had been in cold mash and semolina purgatory. Anyway, who did we get? Cloughie's Nottingham Forest away. Other than Liverpool or Arsenal that was the worst draw we could hope for: they were reigning League Cup holders, had reached the FA Cup semi-final the year before and possessed a quality side with the likes of Des Walker, Stuart Pearce, Gary Parker and Nigel Clough amongst others. They were really strong at home too. Cloughie had won everything but the FA Cup and not far from retirement it was the one he really wanted: game over.

Sunday, 7 January 1990 is indelibly etched in the Old Trafford scriptures. While any true United fan of substance can give longitude and latitude, what else was going on? Camryn Grimes (American actress), Elene Gedevanishvili (Georgian figure skater), Gregor Schlierenzauer (Austrian ski jumper) and Liam Aiken (American actor) were all born on this day. Poor old Bronko Nagurski (Hall of Fame American football player) breathed his last. If you were born on this day you are a Capricorn (or if you are down with the kids, a CAP), so ambitious, persistent, realistic, sensitive, practical and disciplined (if you are at the beginning of a relationship), or workaholic, relentless, pessimistic, touchy, dry and uptight (if you are a year or so in). It was the year of the earth snake so while you may appear nonchalant you are actually quite enthusiastic. Band Aid II (as if we hadn't had enough the first time round) was UK number one although about to be eclipsed that very evening by New Kids on the Block's 'Hangin' Tough'. Lynn Jennings ran a world record indoor 5km at 15:22.64; the Tower of Pisa closed to the public after leaning too far.

In matters of far greater cultural significance, Ken was leaving Deirdre again (or was it the other way round), Phil and Grant Mitchell were preparing to take Albert Square by storm and ITV had networked *Emmerdale* (no longer *Emmerdale Farm*) to 7pm on Tuesdays and Thursdays. *Neighbours* (sadly now sans Charlene Robinson, aka Kylie Minogue, who had disappeared to Brisbane in a lime green Mini called Willy) was a veteran of the 5.35pm slot and this Victorian staple had been joined by its spiky New South Wales cousin, *Home and Away*, on the other side. Much to the chagrin of right-thinking parents *Grange Hill* was still flying high and when Del Boy was not driving a shitty three-wheel van he was falling over yuppy bars three-parts pissed.

What did BBC One have to offer that day?

8.50am: *Favourite Walks*. A weather walk with Francis Wilson.

9.15am: *Articles of Faith*. Creeds and Conduct.

9.30am: *This is the Day*. A time of prayer and reflection for Epiphany.

10am: *O'Donnell Investigates … Booze*. Dr Michael O'Donnell starts a two-part enquiry into Britain's biggest drug problem.

10.25am: *Buongiorno Italia*. Twenty programmes for beginners in Italian.

10.50am: *Europeans*. Chantal Cuer presents a series of programmes about European society and culture as seen by European television.

11.20am: *Spelling It Out*. Don Henderson presents eight programmes for anyone whose spelling could be improved.

11.30am: *Business Matters*. Your life and time.

11.55am: *Snap!* In the first of seven programmes – how to improve your photo album, with help from Jon Pertwee and photographer Anita Corbin in Majorca.

12.05pm: *See Hear*. A report from the Clothes Show at Olympia.

12.30pm: *Countryfile*. How could sewage disposal and the straw-burning ban benefit our precious disappearing peat bogs?

1pm: *News* with Chris Lowe.

2pm: *EastEnders*. (Ceefax Subtitles)

3pm: *Match of the Day: The Road to Wembley*. Live coverage of the glamour tie of the third round – Nottingham Forest v Manchester United, a repeat of last year's epic quarter-final tie at Old Trafford.

Plus the FA Cup fourth-round draw live from the FA headquarters after the match.

5.05pm: *The Clothes Show*. What next? Underwater fashion in the Red Sea. What's cooking? How to look tasty in the kitchen. A search for the bride of 1990; and 'beauty and beast', a report on the testing of beauty products on animals.

5.30pm: *Antiques Roadshow*.

6.15pm: *It Doesn't Have to Hurt*. With June Whitfield. The first programme in a series that looks at a new concept of 'health through activity' with Dr Adrianne Hardman, lecturer in sports science at Loughborough University and Dr Stuart Biddle, motivational psychologist at Exeter University. They explode the 'going for the burn' myth and prove that it doesn't have to hurt!

6.25pm: *News* with Chris Lowe.

6.40pm: *Songs of Praise* from Nairn. With members of the Regimental Band of the First Battalion the Gordon Highlanders.

7.15pm: *You Rang, M'Lord?* By Jimmy Perry and David Croft. Lord Meldrum takes on a new butler, who in turn engages his daughter as maid.

8.05pm: *See for Yourself*. Terry Wogan throws open the doors of the BBC and takes viewers on a tour behind the scenes.

9.20pm: *Mastermind*. With Magnus Magnusson from the University of Lancaster's Great Hall.

9.50pm: *News* with Martyn Lewis.

10.05pm: *Everyman*.

10.45pm: *Dear John*: USA John Lacey is forced into a new lifestyle by his wife's desertion for his best friend. Can the 'One-Two-One' singles support group be the start he's looking for?

11.10pm: *Mosaic*. Sixth of a series on equal opportunities in a multicultural society.

Equal before the Law?

11.50pm: *Shrikant*.

12.30am: *Weather*.

Ah, you have the same problem as me, don't you? We may never know how sewage disposal and the straw-burning ban can benefit our precious disappearing peat bogs. June Whitfield's fitness video may never appear On Demand or UK Gold. Let it go. Let's just assume for the greater good that the 'One-Two-One' singles support group did sort John Lacey out. Does that help? Do you feel better now? How did we bloody cope? You wake up with a sore head for a bit of time and reflection and then you have Dr Michael O'Donnell telling you you're an incorrigible drunk. Some boisterously loud Italian lessons followed by a lecture on European modernity and a rock-solid spelling test will guarantee one thing only: that you disappear back off to bed with an industrial lager top well before midday. Nowhere to go as nowhere was open. Then if we lose, we have the draw to look forward to (which we won't fucking be in) before *Antiques Roadshow*, *Songs of Praise* and *Mastermind*. At least the pubs may be open at 7: 'A double cyanide and a noose please barman and please kick the chair away.'

As we generally had a game which kicked off at 11, I escaped most of the rank TV. It was a big game that day too: a top-of-the-table (but non-televised) clash away against Grappenhall Rovers. We were two points ahead of them at the top and a draw would do us fine: 2-2 in the dying embers. In injury time their 500-goal-a-season striker named Craig Dixon raced on to a fly-hacked punt and slid the ball under our keeper. He wheeled away in triumph only to see the ball stick to the goal-line glue. Paul Lagar hoofed it to safety, and we breathed a collective sigh of relief. We won the league that year by a single point, all because some lazy dad couldn't be arsed to clean up a puddle on the goal line. Small margins.

Was this a portent of more good luck to follow? I thought so until I saw the below:

1. Jim Leighton
2. Viv Anderson
3. Lee Martin
4. Steve Bruce
5. Mike Phelan
6. Gary Pallister
7. Russell Beardsmore
8. Clayton Blackmore
9. Brian McClair
10. Mark Hughes
11. Mark Robins

Substitute:
12. Mike Duxbury.

We were all square until the 56th minute. A superb curling cross from the outside of Mark Hughes's right boot picked out young Mark Robins who stole a march on the rarely flat-footed Stuart Pearce to nod past Steve Sutton. And we hung on. I never knew the clocks went back in January, but they did that afternoon – several times. It was agony alright: you know those work hangovers after a free-bar Thursday when you look at your watch and it's 9.13 and then 400 hours after it's 9.12? And you still can taste the gin and it's 9.30 with the boss whose cat was sick on the carpet that morning? Familiar? Well, it was just like that. Mark Robins has gone down in folklore as the man who saved Ferguson. It's really quite annoying because people think all they have to say is 'Mark Robins' and they are automatically expert on the social history of my football club, when they know treble zero. I can say 'Pete Best' but it doesn't mean I know anything about the Maharishi or the White Album recording sessions. But what about another man? Lester Shapter: the referee?

With minutes left he inexplicably ruled out Nigel Jemson's header? What for? Offside? Foul on the keeper? To this day no one knows but Lester knows. Next time someone says 'Mark Robins' say 'Lester Shapter'. See how he reacts. Hopefully he will go back to polo or hockey or emigrate.

So, was it really do or die for Fergie that day? It is difficult to separate fact from fiction. The players will have known nothing. Ferguson would have been told probably not much more. Only the boardroom will know. Maybe now 30 years has passed we can ask for the meeting minutes and notepads under the Official Secrets Act or its football equivalent? As Sir Bobby droned on about Duncan Edwards over the garibaldis and custard creams, Martin Edwards (who was still chairman after the Knighton imbroglio) may have been practising his signature (as we all do in such meetings) and perhaps underneath scrawled 'FERGIE OUT. KENDALL IN. VENABLES????' If only it was that simple! I always thought Edwards to be a good sort. He is from a family of butchers. Have you ever met an untrustworthy butcher? It takes a loving soul to make a black pudding. I tend to accept his version of events, especially years later when we have all calmed down a bit.

In an interview with Nick Howson of the *International Business Times* on 5 April 2013 Edwards commented on the possible Nottingham execution:

> I had actually approached him that week and told him that whether we win or lose at Forest in the cup, you are not losing your job on that one result.
>
> We had that conversation during the week, so that certainly wasn't the case.
>
> If it had gone on for another season or whatever without any success at all, the pressure would have been there to do something. Fortunately, he did turn it around.
>
> But we knew how hard he was working behind the scenes, how hard he was working on the youth setup. We had to give that time and winning the cup that year was the saviour. We then won the Cup Winners' Cup in '91, the League Cup in '92, the title in '93, the double in '94 and so it went on.

He developed this more in a Sky Sports interview on 10 November 2017:

> We were bedding players in and some of them took time to gel so there's no point in supporting a manager with a host of new players, then before he gets the chance to wed them into the team sacking him. So we were very anxious to keep him to give him a chance to get that success.
>
> I told him his job was not on the line at Forest away. I don't know whether if we'd have gone out

the cup that game and our league position hadn't improved how long I could have gone on supporting him. I don't know and I've always been honest about that. It may have come the day when we'd have had to say, 'Hang on, Alec; I've supported you the best I can but it's not getting any better.'

Edwards had said previously that the death knell for Big Ron was a sense that we were going 'backwards rather than forwards' and that he couldn't see us winning the league under him. He was fair-mindedly applying the same touchstone for Ferguson: if we had have lost at Forest our league form would have had to improve dramatically for Ferguson to be in the dugout on the first day of the 1990/91 campaign. What were the chances of this? We were 15th in the table at the time of the Forest game. A defeat in the cup would have shattered morale and attendances: the Crystal Palace atmosphere may have been the portent of more toxic protest-driven times ahead. Any manager can only survive a certain number of those. The cup was like the beacon of half-term hope: if I play well away at Wimbledon I might get selected for the cup game at Bramall Lane; similarly for the supporters, if they attend the Norwich game at least it's another programme token for Wembley. Without such hope you might play shit at Wimbledon or take the wife and kids for chicken in the basket rather than endure Norwich at home. Indeed, even with the cup still alive the league form was appalling. I was at the home game at Derby immediately after the Forest win where we lost 2-1; Steve Bruce got sent off for cutting Dean Saunders into about 50 pieces. Mutiny was in the air. A bloke on United Road had it in for McClair which was a distinct volte-face from the previous season or two: 'McClair, you fat bastard!' 'McClair, you fucking wanker!'

And the worst thing of all? He had enough 360 spaces to piss on the terrace in comfort. If anyone disagreed with his views of McClair (which I did) they kept quiet. I always felt sorry for Brian McClair. He was respected by the fans in the begrudging way you respect the clever outsider who can play a bit, but they never loved him like they did Robson or Hughes. Around this time, he scored more goals than Hughes; he was more energetic, more versatile, more creative and he was never afraid to get involved when the boots were flying. While Hughes was the favourite son always allowed to do what he wanted on his own terms it was McClair filling in on the left. He would be worth a fortune these days. He was a bit like a James Milner who could also play up front and score goals, important goals too. Was his university degree some form of anathema to the supporters? A maths degree as well? Not exactly the hammer and sickle the egalitarian hoards demanded. It might come as a surprise that some footballers were educated well before Graeme Le Saux bought *The Guardian*.

When we drew at home to City in early February, we were 17th; defeat against Millwall at the aptly named Cold Blow Lane a week later may well have consigned us to a relegation dogfight à la 1973/74. You know the Denis Law City goal that condemned us that year? It would have been even more painful this time around: Denis on commentary was a fate far worse than any free-fall down the table. Less than 30,000 bothered to turn up at Old Trafford to see a 0-0 draw with Wimbledon at the back end of April: I was one of them; there was enough empty real estate on the Stretford End for the hard core to do a conga. It was either a pre-postmodern statement of ultimate irony or they had seen enough. One game to go and we were 16th in the table – only a 1-0 win over Charlton propelled us into 13th. So, the Forest game is probably one of those Trojan Horse things we often hear about but never quite understand. Had we lost there, Ferguson may not have gone the next day, but he would have gone by the end of the season – maybe earlier than that. So, what they say is right: Lester Shapter saved Ferguson's job.

Shall we leave the last word on this to Mark Robins himself? In a MailOnline article dated 27 October 2009:

> Sir Alex wrote a book and in it he was asked if the goal that Mark Robins scored at Forest had kept him in a job?
>
> He replied that if I'd had that chance in training I would have missed it. It was only because I was pushed in the back that I put the ball in the net. Excellent!
>
> So did I save his job? Yes, I bloody did!
>
> It's nice that people think of the goal in that way and that I can have that claim, if you like.

When asked about his relationship with Ferguson post-United …

> I spoke to him on a couple of occasions but I'm not a man who picks up the phone on a regular basis.

He has probably got enough on his plate without speaking to me.

But did he ever thank me? No.

I wonder if he thanked Lester Shapter?

Act 12

Cockamamie Business

The Derby County game on 13 January 1990 was a watershed in my life and times. For the first time, Flynny brought others with him, blokes whose names I have long since forgotten. Before then it was just us two. I may have been the quiet one but so what? For every Morrissey you need a Marr. For every Brown you need a Squire. I thought he knew that. He went on about it enough. But these guys were just the same as him: loud and brash. As they bragged about their exploits with girls and ecstasy I was lost; I could have walked off the train at Urmston or Flixton and no one would have noticed.

That's the tough thing about senior school: there is no room for the cool, independent ones; anyone bringing in a guitar will have their acoustic arses kicked to Sunday school while they listen to 'I Wanna Be Adored' on their Sony Walkman. It's a quick and binary execution: you are either in with the big boys or you're a dweeby little twat. Flynny concluded I was the latter (as I did fine at school and didn't hang around at night) and he wanted more of the former. While they were wrecked at Spike Island (or so they said, like about four million others) they didn't realise that The Stone Roses were all about a subculture challenging mass stereotypes, not reinforcing them. They missed the point and the gig: Phil Collins was at Earl's Court, not an artificial island somewhere off Widnes. I never had much to do with him after that. I was far from perfect in my search for independent belonging: the sixth form was a little more liberating. How gratifying it was to no longer have a school uniform as we all listened to Nirvana in denim.

And what do you do then? I was in with the dweebs now and Paul Brooks was shopping for mackerel fillets at Fine Fare with his mum at 3pm on a Saturday, not in the Stretford End. So I listened on the radio, watched the games on the TV and I studied hard. I also read lots of cricket books in yellow jackets called *Wisden* and some wonderful articles and essays by Neville Cardus and R.C. Robertson-Glasgow. It got me to some places in the end I guess but not Hereford away in the fourth round which we won 1-0. I went to some games on my own which I quite enjoyed: I mentioned Wimbledon before but I also remember Coventry where we won 3-0 and Neil Webb returned to the fray; when he applauded the crowd after the game I convinced myself he was looking directly at me. 'Thanks for coming, Jamie. Stick with it. And fuck Flynny and his dickhead mates.' I probably did need a friend. Sometimes I think I left my soul at Old Trafford around 1990. Maybe I should go back and pick it up if I can wade my way through the inflation-busting rail-fare hikes, the frothy coffees, the pointless foams, the sprays and ices and back-to-back burrito papers. Maybe within the deep detritus of all that nonsense there is a black coffee and chips and gravy soul waiting to be salvaged from 30-odd years of pretty futile endeavour masquerading as 'progress'. Maybe you should do the same at your place of childhood worship? We might all feel a bit better. I was out of the terraces now and into the stands. It was not difficult to find a spare seat for one lost soul given the league position we were in. Stand F at the corner of the Stretford End was the preferred option: £2.80 for a seat (as opposed to £1.80 to stand) made it an easy choice although you had to write in and send a stamped addressed envelope for your ticket. It would add 34p (or two second-class stamps) to the slate but it was worth the thrill to anticipate its arrival during school and tear it open shortly after.

I also discovered around this time that despite years of Conservative rule and chronic underinvestment there was more to Manchester's rail infrastructure than the ragamuffin hard benches of Trafford Park: the soft-top orange seats of Oxford Road, for example. Then take the Altrincham-bound train to Warwick Road by the cricket ground. By the time you are back in 1981 imagining Ian Botham hooking Dennis Lillee off his nose for successive sixes on to the same platform you are standing on, you are at the football version of nirvana. Don't get too bloody clever though. I once took a shortcut too far and used the imaginatively named Old Trafford Football Ground station at the back of the Stretford Paddock for the train back to Manchester; about 300 Arsenal fans had the same idea. It did not end well. With my sedan chair meets test match cricket travel plans, was I subconsciously going all

Tory? Maybe I was back then with my A level aspirations. Certainly, I enjoyed the better standard of comportment in Stand F: a family feel with women and children ensuring good manners and order.

'Fucking Donaghy's playing!' roared the middle-aged woman next to me before the Coventry game almost choking on her Uncle Joe's mint balls. 'Mal Donaghy!' 'Mal fucking Donkey more like.' 'Fucking Irish bastard!' 'Do you want a sweet, love?'

Poor old Mal. He never featured much in the cup side that year. Here's one for all you United fans out there: a KYC ('Know Your Club') question. Please don't look it up: as Mr Capstick used to say at school: 'You are only cheating yourself.' No, I never got that either. Anyway, what was the unusual feature about United's cup run that year? No, you're not having a clue. Give up? OK, not one game was played at Old Trafford. Probably just as well given the atmosphere. It was not like the Russ Abbot song, more like the Cortina after a 250-mile trip to Scotland with a moody dad, an overheating radiator and a backseat load of annoying sisters and on-the-turn tuna sandwiches. Fifth round was Newcastle away. They were flying high at the top of the old Second Division with Micky Quinn and Mark McGhee banging them in. It was live on the BBC again. We had just beaten Penlake that morning in a filthy game and I notched the winner. My treat? Dad insisted we had our Sunday roast in front of the football. He was 41 then. Imagine a 41-year-old bloke getting away with that now? After all that measuring up and kitchen fitting, he'd be lucky to get next week's highlights. This was Danny Wallace's game: he put us 2-1 up with a sublime half-turn and snap shot and then set up McClair's tap-in winner. Odd player Danny Wallace. He was one of those players who was never quite in control of the ball; it was always half a yard too far in front of him. His blistering pace, however, made that dangerous as defenders often overcommitted; he never looked like he knew what he was doing either which at times made him even more tricky for opponents. These days he would be 'good to have on the bench. No defenders like pace when they're tired after 75 minutes, Darren [Fletcher].' He would probably also be 'an option' for a World Cup or Euro squad for exactly the same reason. Maybe history is being kind. Contemporaneous sources, which have to have more probative value, often described him as 'a pocket dynamo'. This means he was tiny and shit. A bit like the most improved player in the Under 11s who could not kick a ball in August but swings at the odd one in April and gets an engraved trophy for it. While you score 60 goals and get nothing. Life is not fair.

The quarter-final was Sheffield United away. Although it was played on a Sunday this one was not live on TV and it coincided with our own fixture anyway. At least it was a home game for us. Normally the cars parked on the cinder track adjacent to the dressing rooms but to keep us informed that day they tore through the sodden turf to line up on the cricket pitch: I bet it took a bit of spin that summer. We could hear every word of the BBC Radio commentary. Our title challenge was entering the crucial furlong and with Penlake and Grappenhall Rovers breathing down our necks, so we had to win that day to maintain our one-point lead at the top. Our squad of 14 was half United, half Liverpool with the parents probably half split too; of course, we were all more concerned with events in Sheffield. That's fandom for you: we would happily sacrifice a league title we had grafted for all season as long as United drew at Second Division Sheffield United (a draw would do fine as we'd beat them at Old Trafford in the replay). Each time there was a corner or free kick we would pause for 30 seconds to hear the latest passage of play. Even when McClair put us ahead we did not settle on our own task: Alan Green always made you think a goal was on the horizon for the opposition even when the ball was in the other half or halfway up a tree. I think we (Greenalls Under 14s) won – thank God no one played injury time back then or we'd still be out there now. We (United) hung on and also avoided Liverpool in the semi-finals. Only Oldham Athletic stood between us and Wembley.

Sunday, 8 April 1990 was a pretty seismic day in the history of televised football. For the first time, the BBC would show both semi-finals live on the same day: so there was Palace v Liverpool at Villa Park at midday and then after a short break for the *EastEnders Omnibus* with Frank Butcher v Pete Beale and the Rest of the World it was over to Maine Road for United v Oldham. Super Sunday indeed. It seemed a great idea to me and to pretty much anyone who liked anything remotely round and leather. Of course, not everyone was in favour: Peter Corrigan wrote in *The Observer* at the time (in comments reprinted in Matthew Crist's article in *The Sportsman* dated 19 April 2018): 'It is a poor and unimaginative idea. The danger of the entire exercise being a drag is not all that slim.'

A drag for who? For him? As he might have to do a bit more work a bit more quickly? As if it was work anyway? I've known barristers who don't like court rooms and chefs who don't like food, but this is a step too far. There was no danger of it being a drag for us in 1990: not when the alternative was *The Waltons*, *Little House on the Prairie*, *Loveboat* and *Bullseye* on the other side. What would you be watching? What was the bigger drag? Maybe Peter Corrigan had an early satellite dish with some real choice of TV or the money to go out for crab linguine and pinot grigio at the weekend. We did not. For us it was a good thing and too much of a good thing can be wonderful. In a truly thrilling game Palace edged out Liverpool at Villa Park. For once John Motson was spot on at full time: 'Crystal Palace 4 Liverpool 3. And Crystal Palace are at Wembley. They've beaten Liverpool whose dream of a double is destroyed in one of the most amazing matches surely in the recent history of the FA Cup.'

I was so invested in that game that I forgot until about 0.07 seconds after the final whistle what the result actually meant. If we beat Oldham, then we play Palace at Wembley. Palace. Not Liverpool. 'Our name's on the cup, Dad.' He said nothing. Europe would follow next year. People talk about decisive moments. This was it for Liverpool. They would not recover from this defeat for a long time. Kingdoms do not disappear overnight: they weaken internally over a period of time before displaying any outward fissures. Within a year Dalglish was gone but the appointment of Souness seemed to ensure the ancient regime was in good order, but sometimes a piece of silver is actually the fool's gold of tinfoil. A year or so later the empire would crumble in the hands of Paul Stewart, Torben Piechnik and Julian Dicks. Women can be more brutal than the city states of Ancient Greece and Rome put together: there is no sign of trouble at all until one morning they run off with the plumber from Newport Pagnell with a note to pay the milkman.

In a *Telegraph* article with Chris Bascombe dated 4 October 2013 Ian Rush discussed the events that day:

> No one at the time was thinking this was going to be the start of a more difficult period for the club.
>
> If you'd have told us after that game, we'd be winning the last title for so long a few weeks later, we'd have laughed. It just felt like a one-off poor defensive performance.
>
> It's only when you look back now, you can see it started happening. There were echoes of the 4-4 draw with Everton in the FA Cup a year later – Kenny's last game – when again we were brilliant in attack but made mistakes defensively.
>
> We were still good enough to outscore most other teams, but you can look back now and, defensively at least, you have to agree it was the start of our problems.

I had just about recovered in time for the United game. Same too for Robson and Webb. It was only Oldham for Cliff's sake. Second Division Oldham: more famous for rugby league, bad cakes and aerobics. Here's another one for all you United fans out there: another KYC ('Know Your Club') question. Please don't look it up; as Mr

Chapstick used to say at school: 'You are only cheating yourself.' No, I never got that either. Anyway, what was the second unusual feature about United's cup run that year? No, you're not having a clue. Give up? OK, we only played one First Division side: Forest. Keep that one to yourself. Here's how we lined up that day:

1. Jim Leighton
2. Lee Martin
3. Colin Gibson
4. Steve Bruce
5. Mike Phelan
6. Gary Pallister
7. Bryan Robson (captain)
8. Paul Ince
9. Brian McClair
10. Mark Hughes
11. Neil Webb

Substitutes:
12. Danny Wallace
13. Mark Robins.

It was 1-1 at half-time and we had been battered royally. We were lucky to still be in contention. Oldham were fantastic. Jim Leighton was no longer as reliable as the Bank of Scotland: his response to the shell shock of haemorrhaged confidence was to lose his near and far post completely and flap at crosses quicker than a ruby-throated hummingbird. Our name on the cup? Yeah, right. Another bit of media-sponsored FA Cup bollocks. Remember the other classic? 'Spurs always win the cup when the year ends in 1.' They won it in 1961, 1981 and 1991, fair enough. But what about every other bloody time? I can't remember any half-time substitutions other than mine. A fella my dad used to work with was having a party for his three-year-old son that afternoon. Yeah, I get it. First, so what? And second, why did I have to go? They were strange times: you were allowed to roam about canal banks and abandoned quarries all day as if Myra Hindley was the wholesome girl next door who worked in the chippy, but as soon as there was an event that didn't require parental supervision and/or our participation per se it was all Sunday best and where's the wet-look hair gel I got you for Christmas? Dad was always one for avoiding the score; it was a bit easier back then but at three-year-old birthday parties it was always possible that the uncle who didn't want to go either would arrive an hour late or so and make sure you were updated as soon as he rang the bell – it would make him feel a bit clever yet still cool and encourage conversation. They made great assistant supermarket managers.

I do remember we both managed to avoid the score. I spent time outside with the three-year-olds! It was the only safe way to avoid the events at Maine Road. Throwing sand about and showing them the right side of the cricket bat was kind of fun; it sure beat listening to the assistant supermarket managers telling us that they would put a hammer to tins of Cadbury Roses around November time to make Christmas that bit cheaper for family and friends. Back home, Webb put us ahead with a header 15 minutes from time. Ian Marshall equalised with minutes remaining. Extra time. We looked Wembley-bound again when Danny Wallace made it 3-2, only for Roger Palmer to take it into a replay. When Marshall made it 2-2 Barry Davies in his BBC commentary remarked: 'What an unbelievable day this is!'

So, the day was a real drag for John Motson, Barry Davies and probably about ten million others. The BBC must have been delighted. Who needs Den and Angie when you have Mike Phelan and Danny Wallace? In the years ahead it is maybe a little strange that the BBC did not break the bank to secure more live football of this vintage; if only people paid their licence fee ...

We won the replay courtesy of Mark Robins's late extra-time winner. No one mentions this saving Ferguson's job, do they? Though it probably did. Mind you, Joe Worrall of Warrington refereed this one and Lester Shapter of Devon was nowhere in sight. Why on earth did they used to tell us where referees came from? Like we cared? I bet they were delighted when all the fan mail arrived:

> Dear Mr Shapter,
>   You are a turd.
> Yours disgusted of Nottingham

And so, Wembley 1990. Back to where it all started for me in 1983. Only Bryan Robson remained from seven years earlier. It was as if Robson had helped me through the journey from the seven-year-old kid with the pickled onion crisps and the playground battles to the 14-year-old with rashes and breakouts and GCSEs. He was still there; I felt he would always be a constant in my life and he has been in many ways: football is an emotional thing, or it is nothing at all. As we trailed Palace 3-2 in extra time with just seven minutes remaining, I somehow felt that we would equalise. And it was Mark Hughes, of course. The ultimate big-game player. The replay was won 1-0. As Ferguson breathed a sigh of huge relief the players partied like it was 1990:

> Glory, glory Man United
> Glory, glory Man United
> Glory, glory Man United
> As the reds go marching on on on!

It was glory, glory, glory after that. Ask anyone in their mid-30s with palm tree hair, beard oil and skinny jeans. That's not my thing at all. This song ends here.

Act 12a

Fish on the Sand

So where do United go now then? In the years ahead? I do like a futurology (it scored you big marks in A level Economics if you could predict where we would go post-Exchange Rate Mechanism) but the best ones are brief so I'll keep it short. I guess the answer is a shadow in the phase of where top-level football is headed.

Apparently, it was Heraclitus, the Greek philosopher, who said, 'Change is the only constant in life.' Well, I don't like it and I will resist it until my dying day. Quite why we can't use paper anymore is still beyond me? Why does everything have to be on a cloud that might explode any second now with the temper of tears or a grain of rice that your wife will move and throw away? But at times I am wrong. Old habits die hard. Recently I was watching us play in the FA Cup semi-final against Chelsea and I couldn't believe how we left Pogba, Martial and Rashford on the bench. Contemporary wisdom was that the game the following week at Leicester was more important as Champions

League qualification was still on the line. 'Bollocks,' I thought. Show me the silverware.

OK, I will: so, Arsenal netted £3.6 million for winning the cup. For the 2019/20 Champions League campaign, reaching the group stage alone secured €15,250,000 before a single game Heineken was supped in anger. Each group-stage win was worth €2,700,000, with draws paying €900,000 apiece. It gets too much for your toytown Christmas till if you reach the knockout rounds: each stage fetches a higher total for the participating clubs: €9,500,000 for the round of 16, €10,500,000 for the quarter-finals and €12,000,000 for the semi-finals. The winner (Bayern Munich) received €19,000,000, with the runner-up (PSG) taking home €15,000,000. That's on top of the money each finalist will have accrued along the way. If that's not enough, clubs competing in the Champions League also receive revenue based on the television market pool, which according to UEFA fluctuates depending on a number of factors, the number of teams involved in the competition from a particular country and the previous year's domestic league position. The estimated pot for the market pool? €292 million. It's essentially the same picture in the Premier League: including prize money and TV revenue West Ham took home £113.4 million for finishing 16th in 2019/20. You cannot question any decision therefore to field the kids in the FA Cup third round on a wet, Wednesday night in Grimsby when a six-pointer at home to Bournemouth is up next. Oh, don't we love those six-pointers? Have you ever seen six points given for a win?

So that's where the silverware is. So perhaps the question should be not why we left Pogba, Martial and

Rashford on the bench but why we put Rashford and Fernandes on the pitch at all. Should they not have been wrapped up in cotton wool in an Ibis just north of Leicester with a hot-water bottle and a good book? This book is not about cold, hard statistics. The point to make, I think, is whether the gravy of commercial and broadcasting income, which is the bulwark of Champions League and Premier League money, will continue to salt the chips of the top-table clubs. In an article in *The Independent* by Jack Menezes dated 3 September 2020 it was reported that the Premier League terminated its £490 million contract with Chinese streaming service PPTV just one year into a three-year deal as the Chinese broadcaster had withheld payments.

I'm no Chris Whitty and I'm certainly no Nick Hancock or Boris Johnson but Norman Stanley Fletcher could tell you that COVID-19 will tear the financial muscle of the game for many years to come. It's not one of those minor strains that will recover with a quick massage and the RICE protocol. This is a Jonathan Woodgate strain: it requires surgery, years off and a full recovery is plain not happening. Is the PPTV contract imbroglio not the beginning of things to come? Sky and BT and Amazon cannot pay for coverage if you can't afford your subscription. Charlie Nicholas, Matt Le Tissier and Phil Thompson have been jettisoned by Sky Sports in a cost-cutting exercise so it's now Super Saver Soccer Saturday with Clinton Morrison, Glen Johnson and Adebayo Akinfenwa. How long are you going to pay for that? How many more pay cuts can the excellent Gary Lineker take before some cheap, burst balloon from Anglia TV takes the hot seat? How long are you going to pay for that? And what about the knock-on impact in other areas? With no top football on TV, inevitably merchandising and sponsorship revenue will suffer. What self-respecting kid in China will buy a United shirt or coffee mug or bed spread if he is not seeing their games? What sponsor will put their names on the shirts? What major brands will go within a bargepole of the game? Matchday income? Forget that: you cannot buy a pint and a pie and a programme at Old Trafford if it is shut. It's all an interrelated mess. What then? What happens when you connect nothing with nothing? As Dickens said in *David Copperfield*: 'Annual income twenty pounds, annual expenditure nineteen nineteen and six, result happiness. Annual income twenty pounds, annual expenditure twenty pounds ought and six, result misery.'

Clubs may disappear into the miasma of bankruptcy. You have heard that before about the League One and League Two clubs but what makes United immune or any of the big boys for that matter? Why does football, especially at the top echelon, always overrate the elasticity of its value and brand loyalty? And what is the game's answer at the moment? To make more matches pay per view! Brilliant! You just wouldn't read about it would you? Except we all have. Out of touch is fine but football's governing elite make Walter Mitty look like a modern realist. And if that's not enough we have the European Premier League to look forward to. Quite how that will pay JP Morgan's fees when people can't afford their discounted interest-only mortgage arrangements and bounce-back loans beggars belief. There is no point in learning when the exam paper has been handed in already. Let's see what happens on results day.

When people switch off their TV the last time and take up jogging and supporting Halesowen Town again. When they hook up Freeview, grout the bathroom and fall in love like it's 2003. On a macro level, you might own a country or a whole continent or business empire but if your plaything no longer gives you commercial or political capital and is no longer cool and relevant, what's the point? You might as well invest in Hantis and Bossaball or Fortnite instead. And they will. There may be personal guarantees and inter-company agreements but so what? That's monopoly money anyway, all on someone else's slate no doubt.

United's wage bill in 2020 was £352 million. In the new normal how will United put 352 million quid's worth of 50ps in the wage metre? If cash flow is king, the emperor is packing his bags and heading for the mountains of Northern Ethiopia as we speak. And what do clubs actually own? What are their assets? No doubt they have mortgaged everything from the canteen cutlery to the boardroom silver. So, they are worth probably very little. You never know, I might end up owning United. And so might you. A supporter's collective may pay £2.50 to the administrators. Maybe that will be a good thing? There's something romantic about Bolton and Bovril in January. Perhaps we can go back to the Louis Edwards days and get a rich butcher on board. Maybe a baker and a builder as well? Buy our way out of the lower leagues? Even if Financial Fair Play (FFP) is still in force and we are earning a quid a game at the gate we can buy big and argue that our sponsorship income in Asia justifies the expense? Any trouble and we can throw rotten meat and sausage rolls and breeze blocks at the Court of Arbitration?

That or just plain not cooperate and spin the whole thing out until the allegations are stale and time-barred. Do you think that will work?

A contrast with cricket is interesting here. According to the naysayers and plain stupid this beats to the unchanging rhythms of our bucolic heritage: slow over rates and big picnic baskets allowing you to snooze behind *The Telegraph* and wait for the inevitability of the draw and/or bad light. Plain bollocks. Kerry Packer was ripping up the bacon and egg ties of the establishment as far back as the late 1970s – sponsors and TV stations attracted by floodlights and coloured clothing and white balls meant decent money for the players. When cricket already had its Champions League, football was still administered by stuffy middle-aged men re-enforcing each other's prejudices, running the game like the Yorkshire Ripper murder enquiry. Sod the media and the TV. And the sponsors. We know best. The great unwashed? Sod them as well. Let's keep them behind electric fences stewing in their own piss: they'll still be back next week. It took football about 20 years to get anywhere near.

And yet football is still behind. Line calls on run-outs and stumpings were referred to TV umpires in the early 1990s – third umpires, match referees and the Decision Review System (DRS) were to follow. And we are struggling still with goal-line technology? So, my point? To see where football is going in the next ten years maybe we need to see where cricket is now. County cricket is dead. Test cricket is moribund. It's all about the Indian Premier League (IPL) and the Twenty20 franchises now. Where will our main man Marcus Rashford be in five years? What about Mason Greenwood? How will his career unfold? You think they will both end up at United as all-time top scorers? Of course, I hope they do, but I think the days of top footballers being tied to the club model may in some cases be numbered; I think footballers will become true mercenaries, not necessarily in the money greedy sense but in the sense that there will be no affiliation or contractual relationship with a club. Why? Because they have no bloody money. Have you not been paying attention at the back?

Surely the IPL cricket model may encourage serious backers to take advantage of the club vacuum and do the same for football. Take Saudi Arabia. They have taken an interest in boxing; why not football? They can go large and get the best players at their peak like Kerry Packer did: not Del Piero and Rooney looking for a sinecure and a swan song. They could set up a rival governing elite to challenge FIFA and UEFA; recruit the world's best 150 players to play for franchises owned and controlled by uber-rich businessmen and corporations: live auctions featuring Mbappe and Neymar trying to out-chew and out-jean shred each other; bidding wars, seven players a side; games of three 20-minute periods; leading scorers wearing canary-yellow jerseys; super stoppers wearing violet caps; Gatorade breaks; live tactics truck analysis; player mikes; pay your credit card bill during strategic time outs and receive a lip gloss and a meal deal cashback; bigger goals; smaller pitches; rush keepers; sofa VAR decisions made by the bloke who won last week's franchise – sponsored spot the ball; nubile physios administering treatment whilse simultaneously advertising red chillies, concrete and reliance industries; live christenings and weddings to accompany the hugs and kisses in the prematch tunnel; ten-minute black bandaged silences to be conducted in floods of tears mid-game each time the assistant tea lady loses her cat; substitutions decreed by franchise owners' VIPs on giant iPads; every drawn match ending in a sudden-death super-penalty challenge; Rashford playing for Riyadh Capitals against Greenwood's Jeddah Giants in the first grand final. Pepsi-Cola and KFC and Primetime would love it. You heard it here first folks. The road show can then move on to franchises in China or the Caribbean.

Sounds dreadful, doesn't it? Let's stick to Bolton in January. I hope it rains and the pitch is a bloody mess.

Act 13

Unknown Delight

A bit of fun at the end as a thank you for bearing with me through all the boring FFP and TV money stuff. This is my Inglorious Bastards: my composite worst United XI from 1983 to 1990. One you can take to the pub to discuss and disagree as long as you socially distance and promise that you will do it on your boss's time? Send it to your workmates in a diary and block out from 3.30pm on a Friday with 'Root Canal'. Trust me it works: no one will say a word.

The pub is actually the only fitting venue for this exercise: no doubt this ragtag outfit spent most of their afternoons in the 80s there when they should have been at home eating toasted sandwiches and packets of crisps in front of Sid Waddell and Eric Bristow.

Before you participate with delight there are a few points of etiquette you might want to consider: drinking games are designed to be a laugh, but we need a few guidelines (not rules) to ensure fairness and consistency.

This is the Magill/United/Rubbish ('MUR') Calculation Coefficient which is based on merit and demerit points:

1. 4-4-2 only please. There was no frothy coffee in those days so live with it. Besides, can you reasonably expect Graeme Hogg to tuck into a back three or Terry Gibson to provide mobility in a 4-5-1 or a 5-4-1? There's more chance of a one-legged fox burying a shite on a frozen lake.

2. Candidates should only be selected in their preferred position and/or a position they have played in consistently. Much as I understand the visceral temptation to select Mal Donaghy you cannot pick him at left-back or anywhere across the midfield. As above, these guidelines are designed to ensure fairness and consistency: blatant attempts at Skinner/Baddiel pastiche will be spotted a mile off.

3. Only candidates who have played 20 league games qualify. We can't include a candidate who played one League Cup tie against Bournemouth in 1982 and then mysteriously disappeared. So, when I mark your answers, I don't want to see Mark Higgins at the back or Peter Beardsley up front. A maximum of 50 demerit points on offer here depending on the number of games played as below:

    a. 20–40 league games: 50 demerit points

    b. 40–50 league games: 40 demerit points

    c. 50–70 league games: 30 demerit points

    d. 70–100 league games: 20 demerit points

    e. 100-plus league games: ten demerit points.

4. Consider how much a candidate cost to be brought in. A one million flop deserves a shirt more than a £50,000 calamity. So those who include Danny Wallace rather than Ralph Milne will not necessarily be marked down *as long as* you show all workings. A maximum of 50 demerit points on offer here depending on transfer fee paid as below:

    a. £700,000-plus: 50 demerit points

    b. £500,000-plus: 40 demerit points

    c. £250,000-plus: 30 demerit points

    d. £100,000-plus: 20 demerit points

    e. £50,000-plus: ten demerit points.

5. As a subset of (3) consider the expectation that accompanied a candidate's arrival at Old Trafford and the body of work he attained elsewhere. Neil Webb may be viewed more dimly than Mike Phelan *as long as* you show all workings. A maximum of 50 demerit points on offer here depending on the expectation on arrival as below:

a. Stratospheric: 50 demerit points
b. Very high: 40 demerit points
c. High: 30 demerit points
d. Reasonably high: 20 demerit points
e. Low: ten demerit points
f. Non-existent: 0 demerit points.

6. Consider critically how a candidate performed in the United shirt. **This has to be the most important guideline and appropriate weighting should be afforded to it.** This is one of only two parts of the ('MUR') Calculation Coefficient where merit points can be awarded. Examine contemporary newspaper clippings. Visit your local library. Ask the old lady who has worked in the basement since the Bay of Pigs Invasion to open her porcine eyes for once and show you the microfiche. Examine all evidence: injury is a mitigating factor; not being able to pass a ball straight is not. The lack of pasta in the 1980s is not an excuse either: it was the same for everyone.

a. Incredible: 100 merit points
b. Awesome: 90 merit points
c. Very good: 80 merit points
d. Good: 60 merit points
e. Average: 40 merit points
f. Below average: ten demerit points
g. Poor: 30 demerit points
h. Shocking: 50 demerit points.

7. Consider (if relevant) a candidate's resale value. A maximum of 50 merit points on offer here depending on transfer fee on resale as below:

    a. £700,000-plus: 50 merit points

    b. £500,000-plus: 40 merit points

    c. £250,000-plus: 30 merit points

    d. £100,000-plus: 20 merit points

    e. £50,000-plus: ten merit points.

8. In 80s tradition wads and wads of gum (preferably Wrigley's) are to be masticated when you are cogitating.

9. Extra points for wearing bulky Adidas (or Umbro) jackets while the choices are being made.

10. Pint and a shot when you agree a candidate.

11. My choice is final and inviolable.

Goalkeeper

'I'm sorry but you can't win the title with that keeper, Martin.' How many times do we hear that these days? Keepers in the 1980s were more functional: they stopped shots and claimed crosses, or they didn't. They never won titles or column inches, not even the really good ones. So, when exactly did the keeper become so important? I think it might have been in the summer of 1991 when after our Cup Winners' Cup triumph over Barcelona we went into the following season as title favourites and then realised we had Les Sealey and Jim Leighton vying for the number 1 jersey. It then becomes very important. Peter Schmeichel changed everything other than that grey suit on *Match of the Day*: before long keepers were saving teams 10–15 points a season, taking penalties, racing forward for corners and cleaning up at the back. Like everything else, though, it has been taken too far: I can take tattoos and I'm not against Head and Shoulders but short sleeves? For keepers? Do they wear socks in bed as well? Maybe some of them know they will never move from the bench again so it's all academic? Why waste money on elbow pads when you are more likely now to get splinters than grass burns and you can buy a soft cushion instead?

Gary Bailey stands out as the quintessential United keeper of the 1980s. He was OK but no better. OK is enough to get you out of this side. So, who does that leave? Stephen Pears and Jeff Wealands hardly played; a young Gary Walsh looked the part at times until injury took hold. There are two obvious choices here: Chris Turner is the first; 64 league games between 1985 and 1988. He joined from Sunderland for £275,000 which was hardly chump change back then. I know times have changed but keepers in my view still need height: Ederson is a brilliant modern keeper who could play in midfield, but he is still 6ft 2 and can clean a striker out if required. In the 1980s size was much more important for a keeper: there was little or no pressing, crosses were launched into the box at every opportunity, elbows were flying and referees didn't stop the fight for a lost gumshield or cut glove. So, we (Big Ron) buy Chris Turner: 5ft 10. Fantastic.

And the warning signs were there. In November 1984 Robson put us ahead at Roker Park with a shot which dribbled past the opposition keeper; we went 2-0 up so, of course, lost 3-2 (for the record we played in blue that day). The keeper could have saved Sunderland's shipbuilding industry and come back in time to put his hat on Robson's strike. And the keeper was? You guessed it. Christopher Robert Turner. So, what did Big Ron do? He bought him. According to Barry Davies on the BBC the shot 'totally fooled Chris Turner'. Well, it didn't take a lot. Well worth a look on YouTube. Then there was Glenn Hoddle's low-flying chip at Old Trafford against Spurs in December 1986 at which 'Turner flapped' according to John Motson on the BBC. This was not an altogether uncommon experience.

Jim Leighton is vying for this slot and it's a tough one: I wish I could discuss the matter with Karen and Claude and then see the candidates in the boardroom. Leighton cost more, and he arrived with more expectation which counts against him in the MUR Calculation Coefficient (Clause 4 and Clause 5). But the MUR formula does stress the primacy of performances on the park (Clause 6). Leighton was better than Turner: in the first of his two seasons he kept 14 clean sheets when we finished 11th.

It was only at the back end of his second season that he started to struggle. Sometimes we need the science: here is how I scored them on the MUR Calculation Coefficient in a close call:

Chris Turner:

Games played: 64	30 demerit points
Transfer fee in: £275,000	30 demerit points
Expectation on arrival: Reasonably high	20 demerit points
Performance: Shocking	50 demerit points
Resale value: £175,000	20 merit points
Total	110 demerit points

Jim Leighton:

Games played: 73	20 demerit points
Transfer fee in: £500,000	40 demerit points
Expectation on arrival: Very high	20 demerit points
Performance: Below average	10 demerit points
Resale value: N/A	N/A
Total	90 demerit points

Not much more than a smudge of eyebrow Vaseline between these two! Don't worry, I don't intend to conduct this exercise for the remainder of team selection! I just wanted to show you that it does work; besides, some of the choices are much clearer cut! I will bench Leighton then and bring him on for the penalties at the end: I can't remember him saving a single one.

Right-Back

Do you remember the guy at school who was a goalscoring machine in junior football? Let me guess. As he grew into schoolbooks and spots rather than height and muscles he settled for a quieter life in wide midfield? By the time the A level examiners had sharpened their pencils he had made the transition to the substitutes bench via the right-back berth. But what if you start at right-back? And manage to hang around forever and a day? You probably get the odd outing at left-back too. Maybe in midfield if there is a wedding or christening or three. You become that guy: the 'utility player'. A euphemism for utter shite? This leads me to Mike Duxbury. How then can we explain 299 senior appearances for United and ten England caps? Well, there are lies, damn lies and statistics. And Carlton Palmer. We could abridge Carlton Palmer's career to 591 appearances and 18 England caps. Does that make him a better player?

Regarding his England caps, Duxbury displayed a refreshing lack of hubris in an interview with the *Manchester Evening News* published on 12 January 2013: 'I must admit I had difficult times at international level. I did okay for the under-21s but when I got to the senior set up I struggled.'

Well, I must admit I saw him have difficult times at club level. Yet, I must leave him out. I can hear the groans and gasps from here but according to Clause 2 of the MUR Calculation Coefficient: 'Candidates should only be selected in their preferred position and/or a position they have played in consistently.' We are talking about the right-back berth here and he was not a bad right-back. He won the FA Cup at United in this position and England caps ahead of the likes of Viv Anderson and Gary Stevens. You know the baby who is happy in the comfort blanket of the hospital but is lost and cold in the one-bar fire atmosphere of the big world? It was like that for Mike Duxbury: it was only when he moved to midfield and God knows where else that the trouble began. I have to omit Duxbury, plump for John Sivebaek at right-back, one of the many Great Danes lest you have forgotten. He couldn't defend for toffee or bacon or Lego. That's one thing but he seemed to have no interest either; in the days when numbers told the whole story of football, they meant absolutely nothing to him. Number 2 meant 'fucking defend and tackle their number 11'. To Sivebaek it seemed like an option rather than an obligation as he meandered around the fringes of creative areas. Anyone would think he played in midfield for Denmark alongside Michael Laudrup and Preben Elkjaer and could do a bit?

Left-Back

Who is the best left-back you have seen? Roberto Carlos? Ashley Cole? Andreas Brehme? Please don't pick a right-footed left-back because that shows you know nothing about the game. Right-footed left-backs (RFLBs) annoy me more than Trump and Johnson, more than Kriss Akabusi, more than Micah Richards, more than DIY, more than the loud bloke on his phone and in shorts at the self-service checkout who realises in injury time he also needs kumquat and luncheon meat and strolls off to find them without a care in the world while you are dying with a hangover at the back, more than the late-night wanker on the tube with his beats and garlic kebab, put together. Yes, that much. And yes again: Philipp Lahm was a shit left-back when he played there. Five words: Phil Neville and César Azpilicueta. Did I say I don't like RFLBs?

They can't defend for a start and, even if they can a bit, it's only off the wrong foot which hardly helps. Any right-sided player just needs to get some paint on their boots and they will have an easy game. It's not just the defending either: RFLBs all make the mistake of thinking they can actually play. They are like seven-year-old sons thinking they are helping with the gardening: they stroll into midfield thinking they can make a difference; before you know it the lawn mower has electrocuted a cat in the next postcode, the rabbit has been stabbed with the pitchfork and Roy Keane has strangled you. Phil Neville is a very good example. Ashley Young was not too far behind at times. Jamie Carragher as well for that matter. Oh God! I almost forgot! How the hell could I when I call myself a football man? Benjamin Mendy! The best (or worst) example of this dirty mainstream art form. We love you, Pep, but really? Who I am to say this but what are you seeing that I am missing? And I suspect everyone else as well? It will come as no surprise that the number 3 shirt will go to one of this truly loathsome brethren. Where are the left-footed pre-Raphaelites when you need them?

It's no coincidence that the left-footed left-backs we had in the 80s were actually pretty decent: Arthur Albiston, Colin Gibson, Lee Martin. Left-footed left-backs are not christened 'Mr Consistency' without good cause. Only two contenders here: Mal Donaghy and Clayton Graham Blackmore. Clause 2 of the MUR Calculation Coefficient saves Mal because he was a centre-back apparently. Anyway ... Clayton Blackmore? He displayed all the characteristics of RFLBs I set out above and more; he was also brilliant at wasting free kicks from promising positions when there were better people to take them: like the ballboys, the half-time singers and the bloke in the pie stand. It always surprised me how Peter Schmeichel largely reserved his stinging bollockings for the usually excellent Bruce and Pallister when there was a far more deserving recipient on his left-hand side (or somewhere in midfield). His suntan pissed me off as well.

Centre-Back

Did you ever manage to penetrate the inner sanctum of the staffroom? I am sure looking back it must have been some form of drink and drug-addled sex shed: all those tracksuits, bad French and whistles can only lead to one place. How many times did you knock on the door looking for Mr Robinson who would stumble forward after a lengthy delay all glazed eyes and coffee cups? On one such occasion we were short for a school-team game after school and I went to the aforementioned to explain the problem. 'Get some dustbins then, Jamie.' 'Doesn't matter if they're Graeme Hoggs!'

I have said enough about poor Graeme in this book. Mr Robinson was a season-ticket holder throughout the relevant period (Stand H) and went to most away games too: he would only miss a fixture if Mr Smith (our art teacher) was away on cub duty in which case he would make sure that Mrs Smith (also our art teacher) did not have nightmares after *Crimewatch*. If he thought Graeme Hogg was a dustbin then that's corroborative evidence – I thought dustbins moved though? This one certainly didn't have wheels in 1984.

Centre-Back

You know when you buy something which appears fabulous in the lustre of the skilfully lit shop and you take it home and it looks double shit? How do you think United felt when they unwrapped World Cup veteran Malachy Martin Donaghy? Donaghy looked solid and custodian at the back for Luton Town and Northern Ireland for a number of years but joined United, piled on the timber, shrank, lost two yards of pace and seemed to struggle to discern that we only played in white away from home. Unfortunately, we couldn't pour some dandelion and burdock over him and take him back to Marks and Spencer on 27 December and ask for peach talc and bath cubes instead.

He was one of a rare breed of centre-halves. Those which don't like heading the ball: just what you need against John Fashanu away at Wimbledon. You know, I don't think I saw him head it once? But it was his positioning, right? He read the game? First yard in his head and all that? Beckenbauer is normally mentioned next so why not? How about Baresi as well? Yeah, right. You know the bloke on the Sunday pub team who can't judge the ball? So, the world and his wife know he can't make that ball, but he steams in and it bounces and then sails over his head like the leg-spinner that didn't turn? And it keeps happening? Week in, week out? Despite all the warnings over the mild and pork scratchings? That was Mal. He didn't help himself either. Back then it was all about perception: if you left the park a snotting, spitting, snarling mess with mud in the bike rack, blood and sweat and tears on the shirt, then you were a bona fide legend no matter how ineffectual you had actually been. Mal didn't stumble across the crutch of emotional intelligence. He strolled in as he strolled out: clean, dry and immaculately tousled in a sleepy, bushy badger kind of way. John Stones must have watched every game.

Right Midfield

Would you want your son to be a top-level footballer? I'm not so sure I would, you know. Not now anyway. Certainly not at a big club. While most of us are two pay cheques away from the shanty towns of Hooverville, this lot are twirling canes around diamond ring fingers: refusing to train, briefing agents to leak to the media and applying for injunctions to buy a reputation they don't have. Maybe there is something noble in our struggles and it is others who will suffer eternally on judgement day? Who knows? Ralph Milne had played to a decent level for Dundee United (collecting SPL and League Cup winners gongs in the process) and had probably contented himself thereafter to a career in the lower echelons as he arrived at Third Division Bristol City via Charlton Athletic. Then, inexplicably, in November 1988 United came knocking. Milne takes up the story in a compelling article by Oliver Brown published in *The Telegraph* on 29 December 2009:

> The money didn't come into it. You could have put any number on there and I would have signed it. I would have swept the terraces.
>
> I would have played in goal. Nobody says no to Manchester United.

And some two and a half years later it ended, in failure.

You know what it's like? It's like being a kid watching a movie, and it's a sad ending. And you start crying. Although you knew it was coming, you were hiding from the fact. I knew for about six months that I was never getting another contract. If it makes a huge impression when United want to sign you, it makes a huge one when they want to get rid of you. Bang, the door's closed. You're finished.

To his credit, not a bad word for Ferguson: 'If you were from a working-class background you had a little bit of leeway. He understood people, he read them before they knew what was going on.'

Tellingly, however, Milne was less emollient when discussing the role that United as a club played in the downward spiral:

It never worked out. I'll hold my hands up to that. But there are a lot of players who have come through Old Trafford and it has never worked for them.

I know what it's like. I don't think the club has failed them, but I don't think it has done them any favours, either.

Couldn't United have bloody well left him alone? He was meandering along at Bristol City, happy enough no doubt. Water finds water in the end and you accept that: you have no desire to get up at 6am and swim until your hair drops out because you know that GB tracksuit will never be yours. Then one day someone shines the Olympic torch and it's 'Where's the armbands, Mum?' I'm sure Ferguson had the best of intentions and thought that Milne 'could do a job' but even back then it did have an element of social experiment about it: throw the carcass into the river and see what damage the turtles can do. Win or lose, it will be a laugh. A bit of light comedy in the dark days. It was never likely to succeed. After United Milne never played competitively again. Who knows, he could have stayed at Bristol City and gone into coaching? He could have been Chris Wilder's right-hand man? Maybe he would have still suffered but it might have been different: he would have stood more of a chance. I'm not sure that the slim opportunity of possibly filling in a bit for a season at United was worth sacrificing that chance; for those of you that don't know, Ralph Milne died on 6 September 2015, aged 54, due to liver complications.

So, I'll ask you again? Would you want your son to be a top-level footballer?

Left Midfield

How many British players who burst on to the scene in their teen years went on to fulfil even a scintilla of their early promise? Best? Giggs? Owen? Fowler? Rooney? There are some who say they didn't ... What about Peter Barnes? I can feel Brylcreem heads being scratched from here. For the uninitiated, he burnt brightly at City in the late 70s for a bonfire or two before fading away completely in the cinder toffee and fag ash of West Brom, Leeds and Coventry in the early to mid-80s. So, what type of player was he? The then Leeds assistant manager Martin Wilkinson made his feelings clear following their relegation from the top flight in 1982 in comments reproduced by Scott Murray and Rob Smythe in a *Guardian* article dated 12 June 2009 and entitled 'The Joy of Six: Terrible Transfers': 'We are not asking Peter to run his blood to water, but we do want to see him get a bit of a sweat occasionally.'

A lazy has-been? Or a lazy never-was? Twenty-two England caps suggest somewhere in between: but still lazy, nonetheless. So, when you already have Gordon Strachan and Jesper Olsen out wide and you need a little more pace and energy for a title push after winning the FA Cup the previous season, what do you do? Silly question: you sign John Barnes or Chris Waddle. No! Of course you don't: that would be daft. You sign Peter Simon Barnes. Maybe water was the problem? Maybe Big Ron thought running his blood to beer and wine would lead us to our first title since the champagne days of Georgie Best and the boys in 67? Needless to say, Ferguson, with his honey, toast and lemon sole, saw right through it.

Central Midfield

I'm going all scientific on this one just to change the pace a bit. What attributes do central midfielders require? Let's start with the defensive ones because although this formation is the good old-fashioned metronomic Roman Catholic sex of 4-4-2, one of the two needs to be slightly more defensive-minded.

As we are in 4-4-2 mode let's go to the *FourFourTwo* magazine and hear the thoughts of one of the best exponents of the defensive midfield art: Patrick Vieira shared these views with Ben Welch on 27 November 2012.

Put the team first

The first step to playing as a defensive midfielder is understanding your role and accepting it. You're there to work hard and to help everyone else, before yourself. The role of the defensive midfielder has changed. In the past it was just about protecting the back four, but now you are asked to do everything: score goals, make assists and defend. Your team-mates need to be able to count on you. And when you're having a bad game you need to know they've got your back. This kind of trust gives you confidence.

Use your football brain

As a defensive midfielder you must be tactically aware. You're at the heart of the team so you have to hold everything together and allow other players to express themselves. To do this you need to talk a lot and use your brain, because quite often you have to be in the right place at the right time. You have to cover the gap between the midfield and the back four, cover the left and right full-backs when they go forward and the central defenders when they push further up the pitch.

Physicality

Physicality was a very important part of my game. I knew that the first contact in the battle was going to be really important. This is the moment when you impose yourself and win games. Being strong in the first tackle says, 'I'm here and I'm going to

try and make it hard for you.' Intimidation is part
of the game, but as a defensive midfielder you also
have to be really good technically. You have to have
the ability to collect the ball from the back four and
pass it on to the front players.

People talk about the advent of the Premier League as
some form of footballing Year Zero and if you were born
the wrong side of the watermark you somehow can't pass,
tackle, dribble, shoot or head; of course, a bowl of pasta and
a shot of creatine later everyone is Johan Cruyff. In reality,
there's nothing new to Vieira's list: these characteristics
were required and displayed by the best exponents many
years ago. So, what do we need from our defensive midfield
man? In summary: understand your role. Protect the back
four. Score goals. Make assists. Tactical awareness. Hold
things together. Use your brain. Be in the right place at
the right time. Cover gaps. Physicality. Impose yourself.
Win games. Be strong in the tackle. Intimidate opponents.
Technical ability. Pass the ball to the front players. Who
is Vieira describing? It's pretty obvious, isn't it? Michael
Christopher Phelan.

Phelan was one of those players who always looked
like he was about to fall over; he also always looked like
he was about to give the ball away. Why? Because he did
both, frequently. Maybe it was the moulded studs? The
boots would have been better on his backside quite frankly.
Another way of telling a shit player. They don't know how
to weight a pass: distance, pace, cut and backspin is for
Federer and co. Phelan must own the world's worst drop
shot in tennis. Whether you were stood next to him or

miles upfield everything with Phelan was fired out of a gun unless it was sliced wildly out of play. What he taught Ronaldo and Tevez and Rooney is quite beyond me. When he arrived at Old Trafford, the pitch was far from the bowling green it is now: it had a big mound of shit like a full-on ridge in the centre of the field. Even then I wondered whether it was Phelan's job to spend 90 minutes each Saturday trying to flatten the beach out a bit for Neil Webb. Make it a bit more Weston-super-Mare than Southend? Maybe it was in his contract? As a footballer he made a great shit carter. Maybe a bowl of pasta and a shot of creatine would have helped?

Central Midfield

Mike Duxbury – see above. Before you choke on your snakebite and stick pencils and Marlboro Lights in your nose and ears please note the below:

Clause 2 of the MUR Calculation Coefficient: 'Candidates should only be selected in their preferred position and/or a position they have played in consistently.'

Duxbury played consistently (badly) in central midfield.

Also: Clause 11 of the MUR Calculation Coefficient: 'My choice is final and inviolable.'

Each written constitution has a despot in denim disguise.

Up Front

I'll deal with this in partnership form. Again, the structure is important. Sum of the parts and all that … You can have static caravans up front if you go 4-3-3 or 4-5-1. When Clive Allen scored 49 goals for Spurs in 1986/87 as the lone striker, he was told by David Pleat to not go wider than the dimensions of the box. Strikers in a 4-4-2 need to be mobile. They can't just hold it up like the target man; they need to play on the half-turn, go out wide, give options to the midfield players on the ball, time staggered runs in between the centre-halves and full-backs. Lineker and Rush were really good in these formations: pace and clever movement are the key ingredients.

So, if you want pace and clever movement? Where better than Alan Bernard Brazil and Terence Bradley Gibson? Do you not remember them playing together? The adroit link play? The darting runs? The centre-halves subbed off with twisted blood? No? Me neither.

I have no idea why we bought either of them, but I've banged on enough about that. Pleas in mitigation, Mr Magill? Brazil got a lot of shit from the fans and may point to a chronic back injury but he had no pace to lose and (before you say anything) unlike Teddy Sheringham he didn't have 'the first yard in his head'. If your heels are always in the ground the yard in your head is irrelevant anyway. The most disappointing aspect? With a name like Brazil I expected so much more from him as a kid in the summer of 1984. Maybe he would bring Zico or Eder with him or failing that Daniel LaRusso? Failing that Mr Miyagi would do: we could do with someone smashing up the joint a bit. Terry Gibson? Not sure what his excuse is? Another pocket dynamo: I swear blind that Alan Hansen once carried him in his pocket for a full 90 minutes at Anfield and he didn't even know he was there. The fly who doesn't even bash the window. Ipswich and Coventry. That says it all. Just because you play Ian Beale half well in Albert Square does not mean you will excel as Hamlet in the crucible of the Theatre of Dreams.

Act 14

And in the End …

So here goes then (I will not bore you with narrative about the subs: like ex-girlfriends they are subs for a good reason):

1. Chris Turner
2. John Sivebaek
3. Clayton Blackmore
4. Graeme Hogg
5. Mike Phelan
6. Mal Donaghy
7. Peter Barnes
8. Mike Duxbury
9. Terry Gibson
10. Alan Brazil
11. Ralph Milne

Substitutes:
12. Peter Davenport
13. Arthur Graham
14. Liam O'Brien
15. Billy Garton
16. Jim Leighton.

Alan Hansen once remarked that the all-conquering Liverpool sides of the late 70s and early 80s would pay no attention to the opposition at all until the team sheets were exchanged at 2.15pm on Saturday afternoon. No dossiers, no team talks, no specific drills in training. Nothing but scrabble and five-a-side. I suspect that this was just par for the course back then but the supreme self-confidence bordering on decadent bone idleness could head up any modern self-help corporate manual. Imagine receiving that team sheet though? No Mark Hughes. No Frank Stapleton. No Bryan Robson. No Norman Whiteside. What would you do? Sod the warm-up for a start! Massage table out; get the liniment and Deep Heat from Alan Kennedy's Adidas satchel, put liberal quantities of both on Kenny Dalglish's jockstrap and then blame Steve Nicol. Laugh about it like only Scotsmen can. You'd be toasty warm in the dressing room before the big event of the day: the 2.50 at Haydock. Warm Harp Lager in the freezer for a quick chill at half-time so it will be spot on by 4.40pm. Mark Lawrenson reminds you it's the Berni Inn tonight at 7 so off you go with the win bonus and the wives and then it's back to Southport for a few beers and a game of snooker before *Match of the Day*.

You thought I'd forgotten the captain, didn't you? Go on, admit it. As if! A captain must display characteristics none of the other players display in profusion and abundance: I've gone for Mike Phelan for his inability to pass, tackle, dribble, shoot, head and hit a cow's arse and/or barn door with a banjo. It was touch and go with Mike Duxbury (who is a very able vice-captain). Duxbury improved a little once he took on board a bowl of pasta and a shot of creatine; his drop shot is slightly more effective and better disguised as well.

The not-so-hot seat can only be occupied by Mr Ronald Frederick Atkinson. Big Ron is emblematic of the whole laissez-faire era this book covers so let's leave the last word for him. In an interview with Andy Mitten published in 'The Set Pieces' on 10 February 2015 he explained his management philosophy:

> Not for a single moment did I ever think of myself as a United manager destined to be in control for ten years, twenty years or even life. Nor did I ever want to.
>
> I had other plans, different ambitions. I was never cut out to be the dynasty-type of manager; an ambition that always seemed close to the heart of Alex Ferguson. That particular notion wasn't ever a consideration on my professional agenda. Not my style, to be completely honest.

Thank God for that!

Those were the days.

Don't be sad they are over, just be glad they happened. I certainly am.

And if you can guess the common theme in the titles of each Act of this glorious little vignette then you are a lot cooler than me; it's sometimes hard to tell when all your love's in vain.